miniature
CAKE
creations

miniature
CAKE
creations

30 polymer clay miniatures

Maive Ferrando

Contents

Introduction

Hello there! I'm Maive, a polymer clay artist with a passion for making miniature cakes.

I noticed that a lot of artists introduce themselves by saying that they can't remember a time when they weren't being creative. This couldn't be more different for me. I had the odd creative moment as a child and have always loved writing, but as far as sculpting goes, it never crossed my mind until 2011, when my mother-in-law introduced me to polymer clay.

Cakes were some of the first things I made. It's strange coming from someone who never liked cakes as a child; I rarely even ate my own birthday cake! But at the time I had a growing enthusiasm for baking that became close to an obsession for making cakes in miniature and for turning them into pieces of jewellery. Soon I saw sculpting as an extension of my passion for storytelling and for creating my own world, where I could make anything do anything. My love for mini cakes is rooted in the happiness I felt when cooking with my grandmother as a child, so for me it is not always about miniatures or realism; it's more about creating a sense of comfort, happiness and wonder, be it through a certain design or through colour.

This book encompasses most of my experience making mini cakes and cake-themed jewellery. I've written it for first-time polymer clay users as well as more experienced crafters in the hope that you'll both find something valuable to add to your creative journey.

These 30 delicious-looking (and smelling!) projects will satisfy your appetite for creativity as well as your appreciation of sugary treats. I hope that you will have as much fun making them as I have had creating them for you. Most importantly, I hope this book will give you give the confidence to trust and follow your heart, because that is at the base of everything you will ever do.

Now, hands on the clay!

Love, Mai

Tools

I THINK THAT TOOLS AND MATERIALS ARE VERY PERSONAL AND IDIOSYNCRATIC TO EACH OF US, AND THOSE THAT I FEEL COMFORTABLE USING MAY NOT BE FOR EVERYONE. HERE I'LL TALK YOU THROUGH SOME OF THE TOOLS I WORK WITH THE MOST AND WHAT I USE THEM FOR. THIS LIST IS NOT EXHAUSTIVE; DIFFERENT TOOLS MAY APPEAR IN SOME OF THE PROJECTS AND YOU MAY FIND THAT OTHER TOOLS ARE MORE SUITABLE FOR YOU.

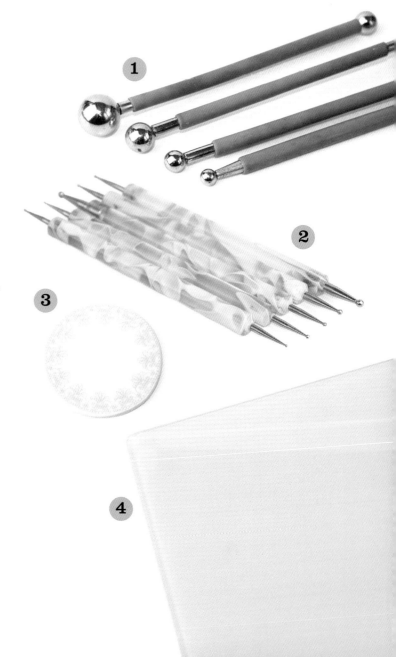

1 Ball tools

I found these sculpting tools among sugarcraft tools; I find them useful not only to sculpt bigger pieces but also to create miniature bowls. I often turn to the cake-decorating world when looking for new tools. Many are suitable for polymer clay, like rose petal moulds and cutters, not to mention the huge variety of icing tips.

2 Embossing/dotting tools

Known as dotting tools in the nail art world, these tools are handy for sculpting miniatures due to their size. The ball-ended tips come in different sizes and sometimes shapes. The handles can also be used as tiny rolling pins.

3 Ceramic coasters and tiles (oven-proof dishes)

Certain pieces need to be baked on the same surface on which they have been sculpted to avoid distorting the shape. For this reason, that surface needs to be oven-safe. I like to use ceramic coasters or tiles, but I have also used metal lids and the base of glass candle holders in the past. Anything that has a smooth, flat surface and that is oven-safe will work.

4 Work surface

I like to work on a smooth glass worktop saver or tile. They're very easy to clean and the clay can easily be lifted by sliding a blade underneath.

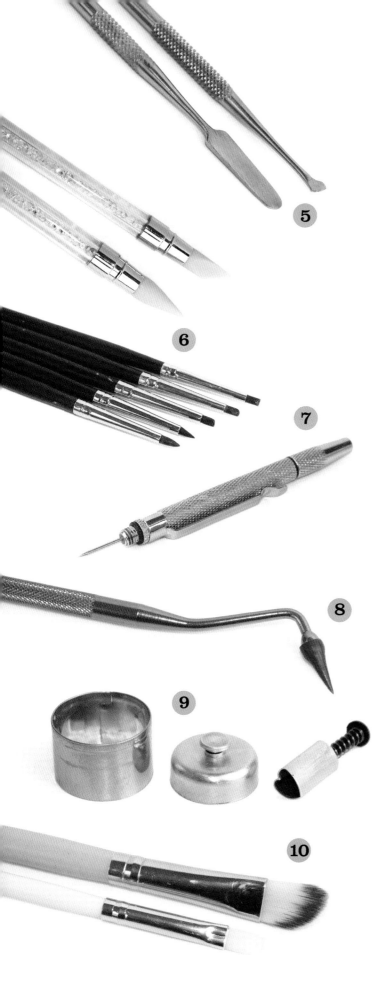

5 Metal sculpting tools

Also known as carving or dental tools, these are usually double-ended and come in various shapes and sizes that can be used for both miniatures and sculptures. Most have cross-hatched handles that can be used to create a waffle-like texture on polymer clay too (see page 176).

6 Silicone sculpting tools

These are my favourite sculpting tools to work with due to how soft they are on the clay. I work with both big and small silicone sculpting tools in a variety of different shapes, typically flat chisel, angle chisel, taper point, cup round and cup chisel. In the art world these are also known as shapers or blenders.

7 Needle tool

Needles are the number-one tool I use for texturing sponges. You can also use a sewing needle or a safety pin; they all do the same thing. Experiment with different ones to see the effect they have on the clay.

8 Gum stimulator/detail tool

Sometimes sold as a detail tool, this rubber-ended dental tool is handy for tracing details on the clay.

9 Cutters

If you're planning to make lots of cakes you will need a set of cutters. If you are buying them for the first time, I recommend getting open-topped ones, since the Kemper cutters, for example (middle picture), won't allow you to cut through several sheets of clay at once. Not all cutters are as evident at first sight. I still use bottle caps and icing nozzles to cut out shapes, as they come in a variety of sizes. In the case of an intricate shape, you can always make a template out of paper and then cut the shape out with a craft knife.

10 Brushes

When it comes to miniatures, I usually turn to the nail art world, as the sizes of the brushes are ideal for painting and decorating tiny food. I also use artists' brushes in different shapes and sizes as well as make-up brushes.

11 Blades

These are useful for cutting straight, angled and several layers of clay at once and for lifting clay off your work surface. I recommend buying a set with at least one firm blade and a flexible one to cut curves.

12 Craft knife

This is a great tool if you want to cut intricate details on the clay. I would recommend getting one with interchangeable tips in different shapes and sizes and a flat handle, as a bigger one like mine can limit the angle you can work at when too close to your work surface.

13 Pasta machine

This is a great tool: it not only saves you time and effort in conditioning clay or mixing colours together and creating effects like the Skinner blend, but also is great for obtaining even sheets.

14 Toothpicks

The toothpick is possibly the most versatile tool you will ever use. You can use it as a poking tool, a texturing tool if you roll it on the clay, and you can even break it in half and texture the clay with the jagged end. You can also use it as a sculpting base and bake the clay on it.

15 Acrylic rolling pin

This is an ideal tool for beginners who are not yet sure whether they'll stick to polymer clay or not, as a good pasta machine can be pricey when you're starting out. Some rolling pins come with rubber bands to allow you to obtain sheets of clay in different thicknesses.

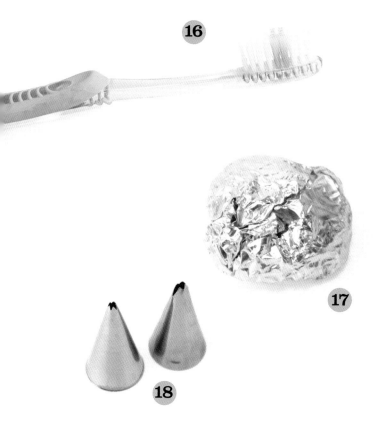

16 Toothbrush

This is the perfect tool for texturing food, and not just by stippling it on the clay. I sometimes like to wiggle it into the clay to create grooves.

17 Tin foil

This is another versatile tool that I use as a texturing tool, a baking base or even as a skeleton when making sculptures.

18 Icing nozzles

I use these for piping cold porcelain; they can also be useful as baking bases and cutters.

19 Clay extruder

This is not an essential tool, but could be useful when you need long strands of clay in a particular shape or to obtain even threads of clay to make sprinkles, for example, so that they are all the same thickness. I recommend getting one with a crank-style handle, as it does all the hard work for you.

OTHER POSSIBLE TOOLS

Some tools aren't as obvious as a cutter and they like to lurk right under your nose: look around your house and see if you can find any of these: crochet hooks, manicure sticks, tin foil box blade, safety pins, sandpaper, empty pen handles (to make circle patterns on the clay), mechanical pencils, nail polish bottles, brush handles and brushes with stiff bristles, old eyeshadows, sponges or mascara wands. What's great about these makeshift tools is that they can spark your creativity and take you in new directions.

Materials

THE MAIN MATERIAL I USE TO MAKE MY MINIATURE CAKES IS POLYMER CLAY, AND HERE I OFFER TIPS FOR CONDITIONING, BAKING, STORING AND CLEANING CLAY. YOU WILL ALSO NEED A VARIETY OF MEDIA TO COLOUR YOUR CAKES AND TO ADD SPECIAL DECORATIVE EFFECTS. NOTE THAT OTHER MATERIALS MAY OCCASIONALLY APPEAR IN SOME OF THE PROJECTS.

POLYMER CLAY

Polymer clay is an oven-bake modelling clay that hardens into a plastic. The brands I work with the most are FIMO® and Sculpey®, but there are many others available Polymer clay can be mixed across brands; it can also be sanded, painted and varnished.

Conditioning polymer clay
Oils known as plasticizers are added to polymer clay to make it pliable and flexible; these harden the clay during baking. By kneading or conditioning the clay before use, you not only make the clay pliable and ready to work with, but also spread the plasticizers evenly throughout the clay, resulting in a stronger and more durable piece.

Fixing soft polymer clay
Sometimes you will get a block of clay that is as soft as chewing-gum. Clays like FIMO Soft, FIMO Kids or Sculpey III are soft straight from the packet, but extremely soft and sticky clay may be the result of containing too many plasticizers. To fix this, mix the soft clay with firmer clay to compensate or try sandwiching it between two sheets of paper to absorb some of the excess oil.

Fixing firm or dry clay
Some clays are hard to work with at first and all they need is a little kneading and a few runs through the pasta machine. However, sometimes you get the odd block of clay that is rock hard and in the worst-case scenario, crumbly and impossible to knead.

There are some products available you can use to fix dry clay, like FIMO Mix Quick or Sculpey Clay Softener. You can also try mixing firm clay with softer clay in a similar colour or a little baby oil can be added to it. Whatever you do, do not put dry clay straight into your pasta machine: the clay will tear and crumble, lurking in your machine and staining your clean clay for months to come!

Keeping polymer clay clean
It can be tricky to keep polymer clay clean, but here are some tips to help you do so:

- Clean your tools before and after working with them.
- Wipe your worktop and pasta machine.
- Before working, use scrap clay in a light colour to pick up any residue left in the pasta machine. Use an old brush or a toothpick to remove any trapped clay.
- Once you are ready to work, wash your hands and let them air-dry or use a paper towel to dry them.
- Wear latex gloves when working with light colours.
- Avoid wearing fluffy jumpers or clothing that sheds fibres, and keep pets away from your work area.

Sometimes you can remove lint by scraping it with a craft knife or picking it up with a needle tool. In cases where this is not possible, it is easier to bake the piece and do the cleaning work afterwards.

Cleaning baked polymer clay
- Superficial lint can be gently scraped off with a blade or wet-sanded.
- Wipe the affected area with a little acetone.
- If you still need to sculpt on the piece, cover the affected area with new clay.
- As a last resort, paint the polymer clay with the same colour to cover any imperfections.

Baking polymer clay
Polymer clay can be baked in a conventional kitchen oven at temperatures between 110°C and 130°C (230–266°F) for about 30 minutes. Recommended temperatures vary slightly from brand to brand, but never exceed 130°C (266°F). Beyond this point, polymer clay starts to burn, giving off potentially toxic fumes. You can bake your polymer clay for as long as you want. As long as you don't exceed the recommended temperature, your clay will be stronger the longer you bake it.

Cover the pieces with an oven-safe dish or tin foil tray, making sure it does not touch the clay, to protect the pieces from direct heat and from any grease in the oven. Place the polymer clay pieces in a cool oven first, then turn the oven on. Once the polymer clay has finished curing, turn the oven off and let the polymer clay cool down before removing it from the oven. Once the cake (or piece) is completely cool, slide a blade underneath it to release it.

Part-baking polymer clay
Sometimes a piece needs to be set before carrying on sculpting it on it or, in the case of sprinkles, they need to be cured before being added to a doughnut, for example, or they'd lose their shape. All I do is part-bake those pieces for at least 10 minutes.

Preventing and fixing cracks
While it's easy to identify what causes polymer clay to bubble, it isn't always clear why a piece cracks while baking. Listed below are some of the possibilities:

- insufficient conditioning of the clay;
- trapped air;
- high temperature or temperature fluctuations;
- polymer clay in thick layers;
- acrylic paint (or other water based/air dry agent) in the clay; or
- metal parts/findings in already baked clay.

To prevent cracks, cover your pieces with a dish or tin foil tray to protect them from direct heat or temperature fluctuations. Sometimes splits disappear on their own as the clay cools down; if they don't, try the following:

- Apply pressure on the piece until it cools down.
- Patch it up with new clay or decorations.
- In the case of a bubble developing: let the clay cool down, remove the unwanted clay, then patch it up.
- Remove all the metal parts if possible, if baking the piece again.

A NOTE ON SAFETY

- Never touch hot polymer clay pieces. Hot polymer clay is still weak and could tear or break if you touch it, not to mention that you might burn yourself.
- Never paint or glaze polymer clay that is still hot. The paint and/or glaze will dry on the polymer clay and your brush before you get a chance to spread them.
- Never sculpt on polymer clay that is still hot. It will first soften and then cure or partially cure. However, applying icing on a warm (not hot) cake will make the icing really smooth and easy to spread.

OTHER MATERIALS

The other materials that you will need to make the projects in this book are mostly media to add colour or special effects such as paints, varnishes and glitter.

1 Liquid polymer clay
This can be used to soften polymer clay and mixed with it to obtain icing effects. It can also be used on its own as a bonding agent. I mainly use FIMO Liquid as it allows me to obtain both translucent and opaque effects, but there are other brands and colours available.

2 Soft pastels
These are brilliant for making foods look baked or to obtain certain mixtures such as melted butter when mixed with liquid polymer clay. You don't need a huge variety: a set of 12 earth-tone pastels should be enough for miniature food, and you can always mix colours together. Alternatively, you could get a bigger set that includes both earth tone and rainbow colours.

3 Soft pastel pencils
I find these perfect for applying colour on baked polymer clay in a very controlled manner. They can be softened with your finger, and you can vary the intensity by applying more or less pressure on the clay.

4 Mica powders
These iridescent powders work on unbaked clay to create metallic or pearlescent effects. They can also be applied on baked clay mixed with a liquid medium such as varnish. Eyeshadows can also work well, as nearly all of them contain mica.

5 Metallic alcohol inks
These are brilliant for creating metallic effects on baked clay, such as baking tins.

6 Varnishes
FIMO and Sculpey have varnishes in different finishes specifically designed for polymer clay. All varnishes used

7 Acrylic paints

Baked polymer clay can be painted with water-based paint; the main medium I use is acrylic paint. If you are unsure about which colours to get, go for primary colours (blue, yellow and red) and black and white, as you can mix them to obtain all the rest.

8 Essential oils

These are great for making your mini cakes and jewellery smell delicious (see page 26).

9 Silicone mould putty

These are useful to make moulds for pieces you need a lot of – cupcake liners, for example. You can also bake your polymer clay pieces in them. The ones I work with the most are Amazing Mould Putty and Gedeo.

10 Nail caviar

Sometimes known as micro marbles, micro beads or accent beads, these are the perfect miniature replica of sprinkles. There are at least three types that I know of: glass, plastic and metallic. They are all fine to use with polymer clay (the plastic ones don't melt). Those with a metallic finish have a coating that reacts with polymer clay and leaves a halo around it when used on icing, for example, which I find rather realistic. The nail art world offers a huge variety of decorations that can also be used with polymer clay.

11 Craft sand

This is great for adding texture to jams and snow in miniature scenes, for creating the illusion of spices, and even for brown or white sugar by simply using brown or white/clear craft sand.

12 Miniature crockery and accessories

I make my own wooden boards and mini displays, but when it comes to crockery and cutlery, I like to use ceramic plates, glass cake stands and metal forks and spoons that I buy online.

Jewellery findings and materials

JEWELLERY FINDINGS AND MATERIALS ARE AVAILABLE IN ALL SORTS OF STYLES, SIZES AND COLOURS. THESE ARE SOME OF THE ONES I USE TO MAKE JEWELLERY WITH, BUT AS YOU DIVE DEEPER YOU WILL FIND THAT THERE ARE MANY CHOICES AND MANY WAYS TO USE AN ITEM. ULTIMATELY, YOUR MOST PRECIOUS TOOL WILL BE YOUR IMAGINATION.

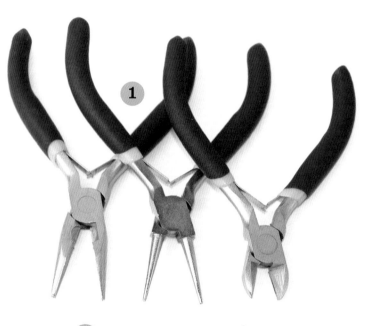

1 Jewellery pliers
I would recommend getting a set of at least three pliers that include flat-nose, round-nose and side cutters.

2 Jump rings
You will need these to connect charms and other findings to your handmade jewellery.

3 Headpins/ballpins/eyepins
These usually come in 1¼in (3cm) or 2in (5cm) lengths. They can be inserted into your charms without them sliding out. Eyepins can be used as connectors too.

4 Ring blanks
Also found as ring bases, these come in all sorts of shapes, sizes and colours; some are specifically designed for polymer clay. I would suggest getting adjustable ones, so you don't have to worry about sizes.

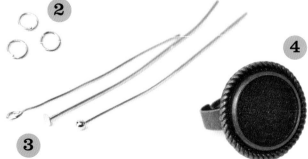

5 Chains/necklaces
Some come assembled in set lengths together with clasps and some are sold by the metre, in which case you have to purchase the clasps separately.

6 Screw eye bails
I screw these into my polymer clay pieces to turn them into pendants or charms.

7 Beads and charms
With the huge variety of beads and charms available, you can add a unique finishing touch to your handmade polymer clay jewellery.

8 Brooch/pin bases
These come in a variety of styles and add a lovely detail to an outfit or bag.

9 Keyrings
A keyring or bag charm is the perfect alternative for those who love to carry a polymer clay piece without wearing it. There are many styles and colours to choose from.

10 Cyanoacrylate glue
To add strength to the bond between the jewellery findings and my polymer clay pieces, as when attaching screw bails, I like to use cyanoacrylate glue ('superglue'). I recommend brands such as Loctite® or Pattex Super Glue®, especially the gel ranges, as their elasticity makes the bond stronger. This doesn't mean other strong glues won't work; I would suggest trying the product on a piece you don't mind ruining first to see if it can be used.

11 Nail art hand drill
This is one of many useful tools from the nail art industry. I use these tiny and inexpensive drills to make holes in my baked polymer clay pieces to attach jewellery findings. Some sculpting tool sets come with drills, but they may be too big for jewellery findings. Always test them first.

12 Magnets
Available in different sizes, these are great for any kinds of craft, not just for polymer clay pieces.

Techniques

IN THIS SECTION YOU'LL FIND SOME OF THE TECHNIQUES THAT I FIND INVALUABLE FOR MAKING MINIATURE CAKES, AND I USE THESE THROUGHOUT THE BOOK. OTHER MORE COMPLEX TECHNIQUES, SUCH AS CANING, ARE COVERED IN SPECIFIC PROJECTS.

BROWNING A CAKE

I like my vanilla-flavoured sponges to reveal a beautiful golden crust when cut, although you can adapt this technique to any flavour cake by adjusting the colour of the crust. To make your vanilla sponges look baked and golden:

1 Mix translucent polymer clay with a small amount of caramel (I use Premo in Raw Sienna) and put it through the thinnest setting of your pasta machine. Try to keep the clay translucent to avoid a dry-looking crust.

2 Cut out the vanilla sponge layers using a round cutter.

3 Sandwich them in between two sheets of the caramel clay.

4 Use your fingers to stick the clays together, making sure there are no air bubbles. If necessary, use a soft tool to push the clay onto the sides.

5 Use the same round cutter to remove the excess clay or a flexible blade if the cutter doesn't fit in the case of a larger sponge.

6 Don't use your fingers to pick up the clay or you will deform it. Slide a blade underneath instead.

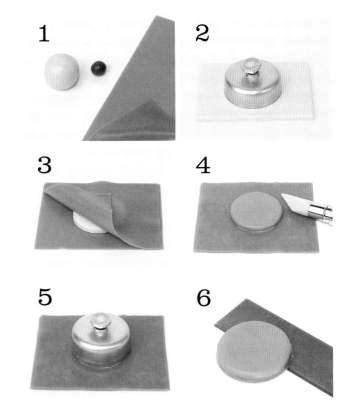

Tip Apply a small amount of watered-down caramel or brown acrylic paint to make your cake crusts look golden. This is particularly effective when you only need tiny amounts of crust to show here and there. To see how I shade naked cakes, go to page 124.

BROWNING FOOD WITH SOFT PASTELS

Food such as cupcakes and pies don't bake into one uniform block of colour: their tops and crusts present gradients of colours that will be different every time they come out of the oven. To mimic that effect, I use soft pastels on unbaked clay and a little acrylic paint, if necessary, on baked clay.

Here I'm shading an apple pie to demonstrate how I use soft pastels, but the technique applies to all similarly made food.

The key is to apply two or three distinctive colours and build them up gradually by applying less and less as you move on to a darker shade. You don't have to add colour only to the top of the food; you could also dust some colour on the bottom if visible.

1 Start by dusting a light beige colour, slightly darker than your pastry, almost all over. You don't need to cover all the crust; allow a little base colour to show.

2 Apply a terracotta or brick shade on the highest areas of the pie, which would have cooked the most in real life. Sometimes I mix the light beige and the terracotta colours together and then apply the terracotta on its own as the third colour.

3 Apply a darker colour such as a brown (or brown mixed with terracotta, then the brown on its own) also on the highest areas but less so as not to cover the other colours. Use a smaller brush for more control over the amount of colour and the application.

4 Bake the pie as usual (see page 13). If necessary, apply a little brown acrylic paint to the crust edges and those areas that would have browned the most. To make the colour a little softer, water it down a bit or remove the excess with your finger.

TIPS ON USING PASTELS

- You can either scrape soft pastels onto another surface or run your brush directly on the stick.
- Always tap off excess powder to prevent getting blotches on the clay.
- Apply the soft pastels with a soft brush in a horizontal position and use a light hand to avoid ruining the clay.
- There is no right or wrong: you can make your food look barely baked or even use black if you want some areas to look burnt!
- Always allow your polymer clay to cool down before painting or glazing it.

1   **2**   **3**   **4**

ASSEMBLING A CAKE

When you have your layers of sponge (either as they are or browned) and filling, stack them in order, making sure the cake is straight. You can do this step on a small ceramic dish, for example, so you can turn the dish and check the cake from different angles.

Once all the layers are stacked together, press the cake down to secure the layers in place. I like to gently roll the cake on its side to make it as smooth as I can. This also prevents some of the layers of icing from hanging over the edge and overlapping on the sponge below.

CUTTING A CAKE

This is possibly the most daunting step when making a miniature cake, especially when you are cutting through a beautifully decorated one that took hours to make.

I rarely cut a cake that already has icing on it, so I'll use the blunt side of a blade to indent the eight slices before cutting it. You can also make a template out of paper to help you cut even slices. Use the same cutter you use for your cakes to trace the shape in the centre of the chart, so you know you're placing the cake in the middle.

CAKE CUTTING TIPS

- Avoid cutting a cake that is too warm or soft.
- The layers will sometimes smear into one another, and although this happens in a real cake, when using polymer clay this doesn't always look pretty. Try leaving the cake to rest for a few hours before cutting and texturing it. If the problem persists, chances are that the brand of polymer clay you are using is too soft to make a cake with or is a bad batch.
- Use a sharp blade to prevent the clay from deforming and the layers from smudging.

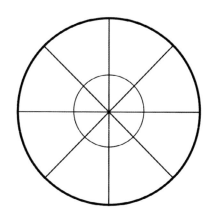

TEXTURING A CAKE

This is one of my favourite steps when making cakes. The result usually determines how realistic a cake looks and therefore how mouth-watering it appears to the viewer.

When texturing a cake, I fluff up the surface of the sponge with a needle tool (see page 9) to make it look like real cake crumbs. It doesn't matter which one – I used a safety pin for a while – but the thickness and weight of the tool can have a significant effect on the clay. Try different ones to find out which one works best for you or the specific project you are working on.

I don't follow patterns when texturing cakes because that's what I'm trying to avoid. I suggest moving the needle in circular movements rather than straight lines or it would look unnatural.

I love texturing cakes and I take my time over doing this because I want my pieces to look as natural as possible. A real knife cutting through a real cake would leave no layer untouched, so I like to tease the icing a little too.

TEXTURING TIPS

- To make sure you're not digging into the clay and only texturing the surface, clean any residue off your tool regularly so you can see the end of the needle and know exactly what you're doing.
- Avoid using unconditioned or hard clay to make cakes with or texturing a cake that has been sitting on your worktop or stored for too long. Stiff clay does not like being textured and you will see bits drop off.
- Soft clay like Sculpey III does not take this kind of technique well, in my experience. The needle can go in too deep and you will end up with grooves instead of crumbs.

MAKING ICING

I use two main materials when it comes to making icing for my miniature cakes: solid and liquid polymer clay. I mostly use FIMO Liquid, but any other brand of liquid polymer clay will be fine.

The solid polymer clays I usually use to make icing are Sculpey Premo, Sculpey III and FIMO Soft, because being soft (especially the last two) they are easy to mix. By varying the ratio of solid and liquid polymer clay you can obtain different kinds of icing that, for reference within this book and in descending order of consistency, I describe as follows:

Buttercream: Stiffest kind of icing that holds its shape.
Cream: Medium-soft consistency that holds soft shapes.
Icing: Runny consistency that doesn't hold its shape.

Buttercream (A)

After conditioning some polymer clay, break it into little pieces and add roughly half the amount of FIMO Liquid at a ratio of about 2:1.

Use a strong flat tool to break the solid polymer clay and mix it into the liquid clay until there are no lumps. You should be able to wrap the buttercream around your tool without it moving or falling off. I use this mixture mainly to ice cakes.

Cream (B)

Take the buttercream mix and add a little more FIMO Liquid until you can spread the cream easily without it separating or looking dry like the buttercream. The mixture should run from your tool slowly and hold soft shapes and peaks. I use this mixture to ice cakes and cupcakes, and to simulate meringue.

Icing (C)

Add more FIMO Liquid to the cream mix until it is runny. If you are looking to obtain a translucent-looking icing, keep adding FIMO Liquid until you obtain the desired effect. This mixture should slide off your tool and not hold any shape whatsoever. I use this technique to make icing, melted ice cream, sauces, syrups, melted butter and jams.

Tip I use mini glass jars and plastic paint pots to store my polymer clay icing.

> ## NOTE
>
> These are the main consistencies I use, but there are many more textures in between.

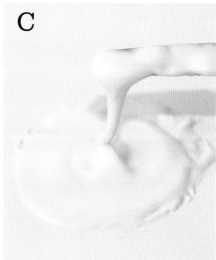

OTHER MATERIALS

Aside from using solid polymer clay to tint liquid polymer clay, there are other materials you can use to create sauces or syrups, for example:

Soft pastels (A)
You can scrape a small amount of soft pastel onto liquid polymer clay and mix them together to obtain the effect of a chocolate sauce or melted butter. Keep the amount of powder to a minimum if you want the result to be translucent as in the case of maple syrup or melted butter.

Oil paints and pastels (B)
Another great way of colouring your liquid polymer clay is to mix it with a little oil paint or pastel. Some oil pastels can be crumbly and may not mix well, so test yours out before applying it.

Acrylic paint
I avoid mixing acrylic paints with polymer clay: one is water-based and the other oil-based, so they don't mix well together. The acrylic paint in the liquid polymer clay will cause it to bubble during baking.

3D fabric paint
I tried these when I first started making cakes: some can work, but make sure they dry hard. Some 3D fabric paints dry flat and/or tacky because they are designed to be ironed to puff up. Most bottles of 3D paint come with small nozzles, making the application easy. I haven't used 3D paint in years, so the composition of these products may have changed since.

There are products appearing on the market all the time, such as ready-to-use fake chocolate sauce, which sounds great. However, they may not be compatible with polymer clay. Always test new products out before using them on your finished pieces or contact the manufacturer or supplier for information.

COLD PORCELAIN ICING

Cold porcelain is an air-dry organic mix of cornflour, PVA glue, oils and sometimes lemon juice or other agents to prevent it from going mouldy when it is stored. I don't use cold porcelain icing very often, but when I do, I either use a ready-to-pipe one or make it myself using the quickest and easiest method, which is without heat.

To make cold porcelain icing, mix one part PVA glue with four parts cornflour and adjust from there, depending on the consistency you want. If the mixture is too runny, add more cornflour; if it is too thick, add more glue.

Cold porcelain icing shrinks about 15–20 per cent while drying. To avoid getting cracks (especially if it dries too quickly), you can add a little baby oil or scented oil suitable for your project. Cold porcelain is white but dries translucent, so I add white acrylic paint or create different batches in different colours.

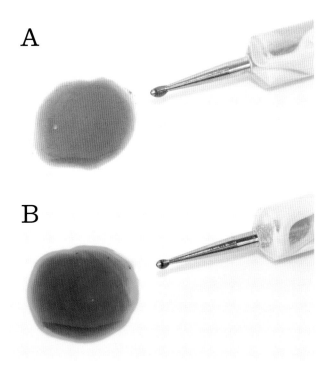

A

B

COVERING A CAKE WITH FONDANT

Covering a polymer cake with a sheet of clay is not very different from covering a real cake with fondant. However, polymer clay does not behave like sugar paste and some things need to be done differently. Here I'll guide you through the process that I use to cover my cakes with fondant.

1 After conditioning your polymer clay, roll out a sheet through setting #5/6 of your pasta machine. Lay the sheet of clay on the cake starting from one side and gradually rolling the rest of it on with your finger. This is to prevent air bubbles getting trapped between the cake and the sheet of clay.

2 Once the sheet is on the cake, give it a little push to secure it, then press the clay from the centre outwards to get rid of any air bubbles.

3 Start bringing in the sides and gently push them onto the cake. Always proceed from the top, working your way down to release any air pockets. You may need to lift and rearrange the clay if ripples and folds occur.

4 Trim the excess and tighten the clay around the cake.

5 Keep pressing the clay onto the cake, keeping an eye out for any trapped air. Trim as much as you can off the edges without getting too close to the cake.

6 Slide a blade under the cake to pick it up and bring the edges down. Put the cake on its side.

7 Slowly trim the excess clay with a sharp blade while rolling the cake.

8 The cake is now covered with fondant.

TOP TIPS

- Firm clays such as Premo Sculpey and FIMO Professional work better with this technique, as there is a lot of handling and stretching involved.
- Soft clays may tear in the process, so I suggest making the sheet of clay slightly thicker than you want it to be because it can get stretched a little while covering the cake.
- Should you get an air bubble, make a little slit with a blade or knife to push the air out and try to smooth the clay down as much as possible. If cutting the cake into slices, try to cut where the bubble is to release air through the side.
- Some clays such as Sculpey Soufflé and Sculpey Ultra Light look like fondant; the latter, however, is very soft and tricky to handle.
- If only the sides of the cake will be visible because you will be decorating the top, use the technique described in the Neapolitan Cake Necklace project on page 194.

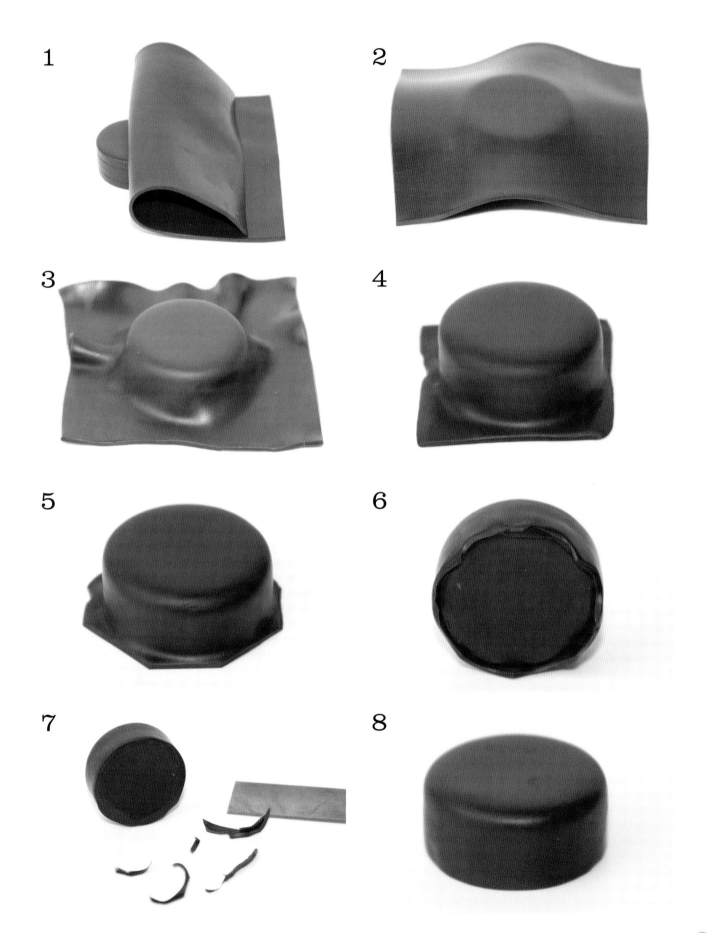

SCENTING POLYMER CLAY

Is there anything more satisfying than making your miniature cakes smell real too? I doubt it. I've adopted two ways of adding scent into the clay and making my mini cakes smell delicious.

To scent my cakes, I use fragrance oils that are used in soap and candle-making; these are highly concentrated oils that come in all sorts of aromas, from single scents such as French Vanilla to blends like Birthday Cake.

One method is to knead the fragrance oil into the clay. However, this can make the clay very soft to sculpt, which is why I prefer to mix the fragrance oil into liquid polymer clay such as an icing mix.

Scenting solid clay

To scent solid polymer clay, add two or three drops of fragrance oil to a ping-pong-ball-sized amount of clay and knead in the oil. Wear latex gloves, as these are concentrated oils that can cause irritation in their undiluted state.

Proceed one drop at a time. The more you add, the softer the clay becomes, making it trickier to sculpt. For this reason, I would only recommend using strong clays, such as FIMO Professional or Sculpey Premo, and not clays that are already quite soft, such as Sculpey III or FIMO Soft.

Scenting liquid polymer clay

This is my favourite way of scenting polymer clay; it involves mixing two or three drops of fragrance oil with polymer clay icing mixes.

It is difficult to predict how strong the scent will be or how long the scent will last after baking. The scent may fade a little over time, although it can last for years. Some of my early cakes still smell freshly baked! Much depends on the strength of the fragrance oil, the amount of fragrance used and the amount of polymer clay used in a miniature. A blueberry-scented cake will smell stronger than a cinnamon-scented bun, not because one scent is stronger than the other but because there is more surface area, and therefore more icing on the cake than on the cinnamon bun.

Some bottles come with a drop-counter nozzle; if they don't, use a pipette or toothpick to pick up the liquid to drip it on the clay. Only add one drop at a time: adding too much could alter the chemistry of the polymer clay, meaning it won't bake properly.

SAFETY NOTES

Fragrance oils are designed to be diluted and should never be applied directly on your skin. These are highly concentrated oils that can cause irritation and allergic reactions.

Read the descriptions carefully and make sure the oils you use are safe to use in soaps. Those that are designed for candles only may not be suitable for use in products such as polymer clay jewellery.

Wear gloves if mixing the fragrance oil directly into the clay. In case of contact with your skin, wash using plenty of soap and water. In case of contact with your eyes, rinse thoroughly for several minutes.

Store oils in a cool dry place, out of reach of children and pets.

MAKING SILICONE MOULDS

There are some miniatures, such as cupcake liners, that you will need a lot of but that would take a long time to make individually. Or maybe you have sculpted a very intricate piece that you would like to be able to work with again. Fortunately, mould putty allows us to make replicas of our originals in a fraction of the time. I use two-part silicone mould putties, mainly Amazing Mould Putty and Gedeo. What is great about this material is that you can bake the clay in the mould, allowing you to preserve the shape.

1 Measure equal amounts of part A and part B.

2 Mix them together until they are completely blended.

3 Take your polymer clay piece and push it into the putty, making sure the putty goes into all the details.

4 Let the putty set for about 20 minutes (times may vary from brand to brand) before removing the original.

A NOTE ON COPYRIGHT

Everyday objects, such as a toothpaste cap, can be used to make a cupcake liner mould. However, making a mould of someone else's piece, no matter how trivial you may think it is, is an infringement of copyright. Unless you have the artist's permission to cast an impression of their piece, I would strongly advise against doing so.

1

2

3

4
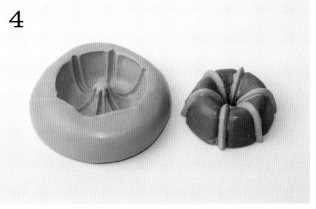

Apple Pie

I WANTED TO INCLUDE AN APPLE PIE IN THE BOOK TO PRACTISE USING SIMILAR COLOURS IN ONE PIECE WHILE STILL ALLOWING THE EYE TO PICK UP ON THE VARIOUS LAYERS AND TEXTURES. TRY EXPERIMENTING WITH DIFFERENT PASTRY CASES AND SIDES TOO, SUCH AS A SCOOP OF WHIPPED CREAM. THE PROJECT ALSO SHOWS YOU HOW TO MAKE SOME APPLES.

YOU WILL NEED

- Polymer clay in white, pastel yellow, translucent, yellow, dark brown and light brown

- Miniature pie dish and plate

- Translucent liquid polymer clay (I used FIMO Liquid)

- Soft pastels in earth tones, yellow, green and red

- Soft pastel pencils in red and dark red

- Acrylic paints in brown shades

- Matte and gloss varnishes

- Pasta machine or rolling pin

- Round cutter

- Blades or craft knife

- Ball tools

- Tapered silicone tool

- Tin foil

- Toothbrush

- Toothpick

- Detail tool

- Small paintbrushes

- Needle tool

- Dotting tool

- Tweezers

1 To make the pastry, mix white polymer clay with a little yellow and translucent. Roll out a thin sheet (setting #6/#7 on your pasta machine) and cut out a circle to fit a miniature pie dish.

2 Press the clay onto the dish with your fingers and/ or a ball tool. You may need a little liquid polymer clay to make it stick.

Tip Polymer clay doesn't always stick to metal (which can be useful if something didn't go as planned), so if you want the pie to stay on this pie dish permanently, use a little cyanoacrylate glue to stick it back in once it has been baked.

3 To make the cooked apples, mix yellow and translucent clay (and/or a little light brown). Roll out a thin strand, flatten it slightly and cut lots of thin slices. Use firm clay for the slices to hold the shape in the next step.

4 Mix the slices with liquid polymer clay and soft pastels in beige and terracotta shades. Use a tapered silicone tool to gently mix everything together to avoid damaging the slices. If you used soft clay for the cooked apples, let it cool down before slicing it and mixing it.

5 Apply the apple mixture to the dish and gently nudge the slices into place.

6 Cut out a circle of the pastry polymer clay mix and press a sheet of crumpled foil onto it to texture it. I also gently rolled a ball of tin foil on it and pressed a toothbrush into it to add finer texture.

7 Place the lid on the pie and use a toothpick to indent the crust; this will also help secure the lid down.

1

4

8 Using a detail tool, trace diagonal lines on the crust. Use a toothbrush to add a little more texture and a detail tool to poke tiny holes here and there.

9 To make the pie look baked and golden, dust soft pastels in at least two different shades so that you can create a gradient (see page 19).

10 Use a knife to make some slits in the pie and a needle tool to fluff them up a little.

11 Cut a small circle out of the pastry mix and trim tiny triangles off the top and bottom to make the apple shape. Make a tiny leaf and texture both. Add them to the pie, bonding with a little liquid polymer clay, then brown them with soft pastels. Cut out a slice and texture the inside of the pastry with a needle tool; texture the apples too if you want. You can add extra pieces of apple and juice oozing out of the pie. Bake (see page 13).

12 Once the pie is cool, add the last few touches with brown acrylic paints. Glaze the apples with gloss varnish and the pastry with either matte or a little gloss varnish.

13 To make some apples to go with the pie, mix white clay with a little yellow and translucent to obtain a pale yellow colour. Roll the pieces of clay into balls and pinch the bottoms as you turn them so that they are narrower. Squeeze the top and base of the apple so that it doesn't elongate too much and to keep the rounded shape.

14 Use a dotting tool to mark the top of the apple to start with so you know it is more or less in the middle, then use the same tool to emphasize the hole. Move on to a slightly smaller ball tool to make a slightly deeper hole and a third smaller ball tool if you want. Then go back to the first ball tool to soften the edges of the hole and make the dip more rounded and natural-looking.

15 You can use the same technique for the bottom of the apple only using smaller ball tools and/or a needle or dotting tool to mark a cross, then soften the lines with your fingers or a dotting tool.

16 To blush the apples and create a foundation colour, mix yellow soft pastels with a tiny amount of green and apply that all over the apples. Next, apply the red colour on the top and bottom of the apples. Different kinds of apples can be used to make pies, so feel free to use different colours to blush your miniature apples.

Tip I like to stipple the colour gently onto the clay instead of brushing it as that can scrape the colour away and scratch the clay.

17 Using a sharp blade, cut one (or more) apple in half. Cut the apple downwards; if it loses the shape a bit, make it round again. Use a toothbrush to texture the inside and a needle tool to run some gentle lines down the middle.

12

Use a small dotting tool to make space for the seeds, which you can make out of tiny teardrops of brown clay.

18 Take some pre-baked very thin strands of light brown clay and trim them into little pieces. Pick them up with tweezers and dip the end in a little liquid polymer clay, then push them into the apples to make the stalks. Bake all the apples.

19 Use a little warm brown acrylic paint to darken the inside of the apple halves. Use the same colour to add shading to the top and bottom of the apples.

20 To further blush the apples, use soft pastel pencils: they offer control and precision and you can vary the intensity by applying more or less pressure. Start by tracing short lines around the top of the apple, then use your finger and/or a rubber tool to blend the colour down and towards the stalk at the top. Once the colour is blended, you can go back in with the pencil to create more strokes and even use darker colours.

21 Stick your apples on the end of a needle tool or safety pin so you can glaze them. This will protect the soft pastels during the next step; leave the area around the stalk unglazed for now.

22 Add the last few touches to the apples using a little brown acrylic paint to shade the stalks and the inside of the top and bottom. Now you can glaze that area. Let dry completely.

Victoria Sponge Cake

NAMED AFTER QUEEN VICTORIA, THIS SPONGE CAKE IS A STAPLE OF ENGLISH AFTERNOON TEA AND PICNICS IN THE RAIN! IN THIS PROJECT WE'LL BE REPLICATING THE ORIGINAL RECIPE THAT HAS A RASPBERRY JAM AND WHIPPED DOUBLE CREAM FILLING, BUT FEEL FREE TO CUSTOMIZE YOUR VERSION OF THIS CLASSIC ACCORDING TO YOUR TASTE. ADD STRAWBERRY SLICES FOR A MORE MODERN TAKE.

YOU WILL NEED

- Polymer clay in white, yellow, translucent, translucent red, alizarin crimson and leaf green

- Liquid polymer clay (I used FIMO Liquid)

- Soft pastels in browns and dark red

- Clear craft sand

- Acrylic paint in white

- Gloss varnish

- Pasta machine or rolling pin

- Round cutter

- Toothbrush

- Needle tool

- Blades

- Tapered silicone tool

- Toothpick

- Small paintbrushes

- Dotting tool

- Tweezers

- Ovenproof dish

1 To make the Victoria sponge cake mix, blend white clay with a little yellow to obtain a pastel yellow tone. Once you're happy with that colour, add equal amounts of translucent polymer clay, then adjust the amount of translucent according to taste. The translucent clay gives the sponge a moist look.

Tip If you add too much translucent clay and the cake looks greasy rather than moist, add a little more pastel yellow clay.

2 Put the clay through the thickest setting of your pasta machine and use the round cutter to cut out a circle to make the bottom layer.

3 To make the top layer of sponge, stack two sheets, one thinner than the other (settings #1 and #4), and cut out the shape.

4 Thin out the edges with your finger.

5 Remove the excess clay using the same cutter.

6 Follow the steps for browning a cake on page 18. Place your sponges on an oven-proof dish (like my ceramic coaster) and texture them with a toothbrush. This way you can use the dish like a turntable and see what you're doing.

7 When texturing the top sponge, wiggle the end of the toothbrush right where the cake dips to create a more realistic texture.

8 Fluff up the edges of the sponge using a needle tool.

9 Cut out a couple of slices of the top sponge.

10 Use the top sponge as a template to cut the same size pieces from the bottom layer.

11 Texture the inside of the sponge with a needle tool.

1

4

7

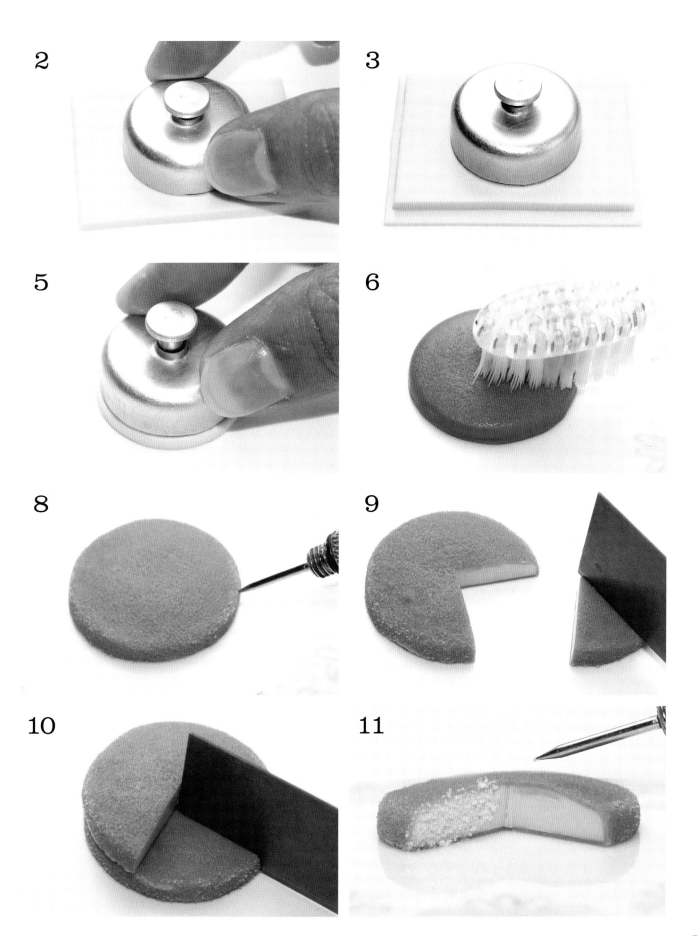

2

3

5

6

8

9

10

11

12 Make some white cream (see page 22), spread a layer on the bottom sponge and part-bake for 10 minutes (see page 13).

13 To make the strawberry jam, chop up red translucent clay, add a little clear craft sand, dark red soft pastels and liquid polymer clay. The craft sand will give the liquid polymer clay a little texture, similar to jam.

14 Spread the jam on the baked and cool icing, and drag some of the jam down with a tapered silicone tool onto the sponge or oozing out from the sides.

15 Add the top layer of sponge and use a needle tool to blend some of it onto the jam. Part-bake for 10 minutes.

16 Once cool, stipple a little white acrylic paint on the top sponge to create the illusion of icing sugar.

17 To make the strawberries, mix polymer clay in red and alizarin crimson.

18 Make tiny balls and place them on the end of a toothpick as you shape them. Use a needle tool to create the effect of seeds. Carefully remove the strawberries from the toothpick as you turn it and part-bake them for 10 minutes. You could also bake them on the toothpick on a base made of scrunched-up tin foil.

19 For the strawberry leaves, use a dotting tool to flatten and break small pieces of leaf-green clay.

20 Fill the baked and cool strawberries with clay, bonding with liquid polymer clay, and add the leaves.

21 Dip the strawberries in a little liquid polymer clay, arrange them on the cake and bake one last time for 30 minutes. Glaze the jam and the strawberries.

13

14

16

17

19

20

21

Blueberry Cake

A MINIATURE CAKE COLLECTION WOULD NOT BE COMPLETE WITHOUT A BLUEBERRY CAKE. IN THIS PROJECT YOU'LL LEARN THE BASIC TECHNIQUES THAT WILL ENABLE YOU TO CREATE OTHER FRUITY CAKES WITH JUICY-LOOKING SPONGES.

YOU WILL NEED

- Polymer clay in Victoria sponge cake mix (see page 36), white, yellow and dark blue

- Liquid polymer clay (I used FIMO Liquid)

- Talcum powder

- Acrylic paints in blue, purple and fuchsia

- Gloss varnish

- Blades/craft knife

- Mini ceramic plates

- Pasta machine or rolling pin

- Round cutter

- Needle tool

- Toothbrush

- Toothpick or flat tool

- Tweezers

- Small paintbrushes

1 To make the sponges, cut out three circles using the Victoria sponge cake mix and brown them as on page 18. Mix white clay with a little yellow to obtain a very pale yellow or off-white, roll out a thin sheet (setting #5 on your pasta machine) and cut out two circles to make the icing.

2 Stack the layers and cut a couple of slices.

3 Fluff up the sponge using a needle tool.

4 Use a little liquid polymer clay to stick the slices to ceramic plates and texture them as well. Use a toothbrush to texture the bottom of the slice if laying on its side.

5 Take some dark blue clay and use a needle tool to break off small pieces. Poke little holes in the sponge and push the blue clay in. Fluff up the surrounding sponge so that it looks more natural. Part-bake for 1.5 minutes (see page 13).

Tip Try varying the size, shape and depth of the blueberries to create a more natural effect.

6 Roll out a thin strand of the same dark blue clay and cut out as many pieces as you want whole blueberries. Roll them into balls and use a needle tool to poke a tiny hole, flicking the edges outwards to create a sort of star shape.

7 Dust the blueberries with a little talcum powder. Carefully shake the dish to coat the clay instead of moving them around with a tool to avoid deforming them. Part-bake.

8 Once cool, gently rub the blueberries between your fingers to remove any excess powder.

9 Take the same pale yellow clay and mix it with liquid polymer clay to make the buttercream. Spread it on the cake and slices. You can use a flat tool or a toothpick to smooth the surface and create palette-knife strokes.

1

5

10 Run a toothpick down the edges to neaten up the icing and create the illusion of a knife cutting through the cake.

11 Use tweezers to add the baked, cool blueberries to the cake and bake again for 30 minutes.

12 To make the blueberries look juicy, mix acrylic paints in blue, purple and fuchsia. Apply a wash of colour on and around the blueberries, soaking up the excess with a clean brush. You can vary the colours slightly and use a more fuchsia-looking tone where the juice wouldn't be so concentrated for a more natural look. Apply a thin coat of glaze to the frosting and allow to dry.

Tip Apply a small amount of glaze to the sponge and fruit to make it look even moister; do this in a stippling motion to avoid a flat-looking surface.

2

3

4

6

7

8

9

10

11

12

Black Forest Gateau

THIS PROJECT WAS INSPIRED BY A MORE MODERN TAKE ON THE BLACK FOREST GATEAU, BUT YOU CAN USE OTHER TECHNIQUES IN THIS BOOK TO CUSTOMIZE THE DECORATIONS ACCORDING TO YOUR TASTE AND GO AS TRADITIONAL OR AS MODERN AS YOU LIKE.

YOU WILL NEED

- Polymer clay in light brown (I used Premo in Raw Sienna), white, alizarin crimson, red, and translucent

- Soft pastels in browns and red

- Liquid polymer clay (I used FIMO Liquid)

- Jewellery wire, 0.40mm/26 AWG

- Acrylic paints in green, brown and dark red

- Gloss varnish

- Pasta machine or rolling pin

- Round cutter

- Toothbrush

- Needle tool

- Dotting tool

- Detail tool

- Toothpick

- Tweezers

- PVA glue

- Small paintbrushes

1 Roll out a sheet of light brown polymer clay through one of the thickest settings of your pasta machine and cut out three circles. Texture them with a toothbrush.

2 Dust the sponges with dark brown soft pastels to make the cake look baked. You don't need to brown all the tops as only one layer will be visible, but you do have to brown all the sides.

3 Use a needle tool to texture the edges of the sponges and make them a little fluffier and to create tiny holes here and there.

4 Make some white cream mix (see page 22) and spread it on the first layer of sponge.

Tip Don't spread the cream all the way to the edge: when you add the other layers and push them down, the cream will spread out.

5 Mix alizarin crimson with a little red clay to make it lighter and roll out a thin strand. Cut out small pieces and roll them into balls to make the cherries. Poke a little hole into some of them and crush a few, then place them on the cream. You can add them wherever you want, but as those in the centre won't be visible, you can just stick to the edges.

6 Mix liquid polymer clay with a little red and brown soft pastels to create the cherry syrup and spread it on the cherries, dragging some of it down the side of the sponge too if you like. Add the next layer of sponge and add the rest of the cream and cherries.

7 To make whole fresh cherries, mix red with some translucent clay. Roll the clay into a thin strand, cut off some pieces and roll them into balls. Trim pieces of thin jewellery wire, dip one end in a little liquid polymer clay and push them into the cherries for the stalks. Part-bake (see page 13).

8 Make some brown cream/icing mix. Spread on the top sponge layer and add the cherries. Bake.

9 Dab a little PVA glue on the end of the cherry stalks and let dry.

10 Use green acrylic paints to paint the stalks and the ends brown, blending the colour down.

11 Add a wash of dark red and brown acrylic paint to the whole cherries to create some shading and a little variety. Glaze the chocolate and cherries.

Chocolate Cake

A CHOCOLATE CAKE IS ONE OF THE TRICKIEST CAKES TO MAKE IN MINIATURE. A REAL CAKE IS BIG ENOUGH FOR US TO DISCERN THE SPONGE FROM THE ICING, EVEN IF THEY ARE SIMILAR IN COLOUR. BUT IN MINIATURES, IF THERE ISN'T ENOUGH CONTRAST, COLOURS TEND TO BLEND INTO EACH OTHER AND SOME OF THE MAGIC IS LOST. THE KEY IS TO KEEP EITHER THE SPONGE OR THE ICING LIGHTER SO THAT THEY'RE EASILY DISCERNIBLE.

YOU WILL NEED

- Polymer clay in dark brown (I used Premo in Burnt Umber), white and light brown

- Liquid polymer clay (I used FIMO Liquid)

- Mini ceramic plates

- Soft pastels in brown

- Gloss varnish

- Pasta machine or rolling pin

- Round cutter

- Blades

- Dotting tool

- Needle tool

- Mini serrated scraper

- Toothpick

- Detail tool

- Small paintbrushes

1 To make the sponges, roll out a thick sheet of dark brown polymer clay and cut out five circles. For the icing, mix that colour with white to obtain a lighter tone that looks more like chocolate mousse. Then roll out a thinner sheet (setting #5/#6 on your pasta machine) and cut out four circles.

2 Stack all the layers together and use a blade to cut out a couple of slices.

3 Texture the sponges and slices with a needle tool.

4 Press the slices onto ceramic plates, bonding with a little liquid polymer clay. Part-bake the cake and slices for 15 minutes (see page 13).

5 Make the buttercream (see page 22) out of the same mousse colour and spread a generous amount on the side of the cake only. Using a mini serrated scraper, remove the excess icing by slowly turning the dish. If you need to stop, do so gently and clean the scraper before carrying on. Neaten up the edges with a toothpick and bake the cake and slices for another 10–15 minutes.

Tip To make a mini serrated scraper, trim the metal blade from a tin foil or cling film box, sandwich it between two sheets of clay and bake for 30 minutes.

6 Cover the top of the cake with more icing and part-bake.

7 To make the melted chocolate, mix dark brown polymer clay with liquid polymer clay to an icing consistency and spread it on top of the cake. Use a dotting tool to drag the clay down to create the drips.

8 Use a paintbrush to blend the melted chocolate into the buttercream frosting.

9 Make a thin strand out of light brown clay, cover in warm brown soft pastels and bake for 10 minutes. Chop it up to create roasted hazelnuts.

1

4

7

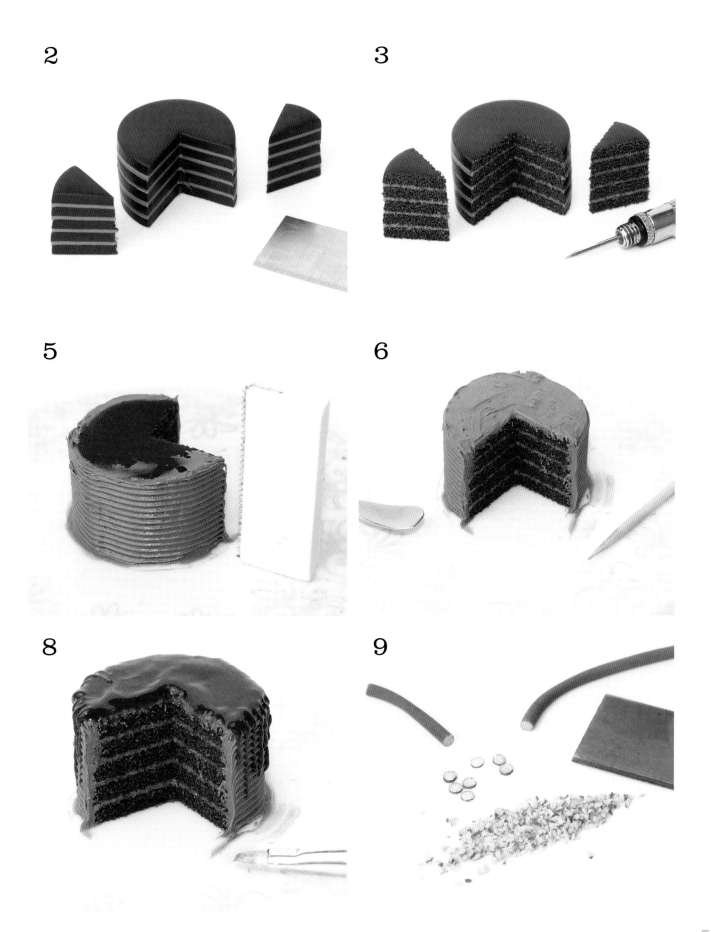

10 Sprinkle the chopped nuts over the cake and bake again for 10–15 minutes.

11 Roll out a strand of the same mousse colour and cut out eight pieces. Roll them into balls and pinch and turn the tops on your work surface to create mini 'mountain' shapes which you will turn into swirls of buttercream for the top of the cake.

12 Use a dotting tool to trace diagonal lines from the base to the top of the mountain shape. Once you finish doing this, run the tool down the lines again from the top to the bottom, because the shape can get a little elongated by working only upwards. Make another seven in the same way.

13 Dab a little liquid polymer clay on the cake and cake slices, then place your swirls of chocolate mousse. Go through the lines again to get the final shape and to secure the base to the baked cake.

14 Roll out a thin strand of the mousse clay and cut out small pieces. Roll them into little balls and then into teardrop shapes.

15 Flatten them a little, especially at the narrow end. Using a detail tool, trace a line down the centre of the teardrop shape, then another one on the right and one on the left, both converging towards the middle. You should have three lines and five sections.

16 Brush a little liquid polymer clay around the bottom edge of the cakes and place the smaller buttercream decorations. If any of them are left sticking out from the edges, trim them, as that's what a real knife would have done. Bake for 30 minutes. Once cool, glaze the melted chocolate.

10

13a

15

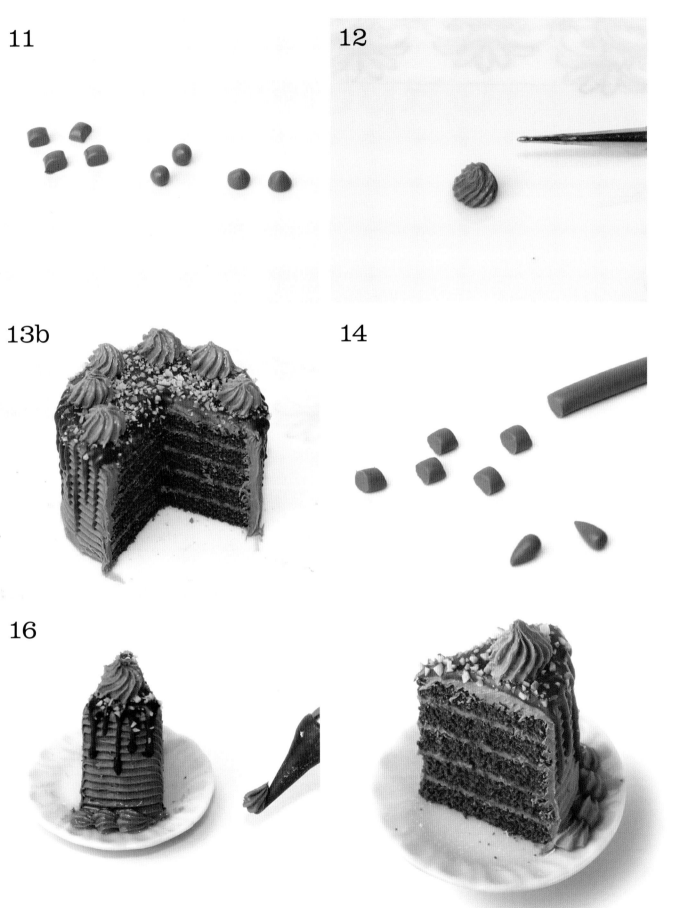

11

12

13b

14

16

Cupcakes

A MINIATURE OF A MINIATURE! IN THIS PROJECT I'LL BE SHOWING YOU HOW TO MAKE CLASSIC VANILLA AND CHOCOLATE CUPCAKES, BUT YOU CAN MAKE ANY FLAVOUR YOU WANT. TURN THE CUPCAKES INTO MUFFINS SIMPLY BY USING MORE CLAY ON TOP.

YOU WILL NEED

- Polymer clay in translucent, yellow, white, dark brown (I used Premo in Burnt Umber) and scrap clay

- Soft pastels in beige

- Acrylic paints in beige, raw sienna, burnt sienna, caramel and white

- Flat chisel silicone sculpting tools (small and large)

- Silicone mould putty

- Toothbrush

- Soft brush

- Small paintbrushes

1 Take some scrap clay in the size you want your cupcake liner to be, shape it into a cylinder and flatten it slightly.

2 Use a large flat chisel (or other flat tool) to shape the sides at an angle. To make a straight liner, just keep the tool straight.

3 Take a small flat chisel and push it straight into the clay to create the creases. Use the same tool to push the clay at angles to create ridges on every crease.

4 When you're happy with the look, bake the cupcake (see page 13) and make a mould as described on page 27.

5 To make a vanilla cupcake, I use two variations of the same colour clay. The Victoria sponge cake mix (see page 36) with a little more translucent clay (the ball on the right) will form the top of the cupcake, and translucent clay tinted with a little Victoria sponge cake mix will be used for the base. Note: This is to make a cupcake with a translucent white liner, but you can make the liner in any colour you want.

6 Take your cupcake mould and use the tinted translucent mix to fill the mould.

Tip Even if you are using the same colour to make both parts of the cupcake, fill the mould to the top first and then add the top. This is to prevent the mould from texturing the top of the cupcake.

7 Take a small amount of the second colour and shape it into a ball. Place it on the cupcake and flatten it, giving it a domed shape. Muffins tend to be bigger and bulgier than cupcakes, so add more if making muffins.

1

5

8 Use a toothbrush to texture the clay. A toothbrush is enough if you'll be applying icing, because only a small portion of the cupcake will be visible, but create more detail such as tears and dips if leaving the cupcakes as they are or if you are making muffins.

9 Use a small soft brush to apply a light dusting of beige soft pastels. Part-bake if applying icing; otherwise bake completely.

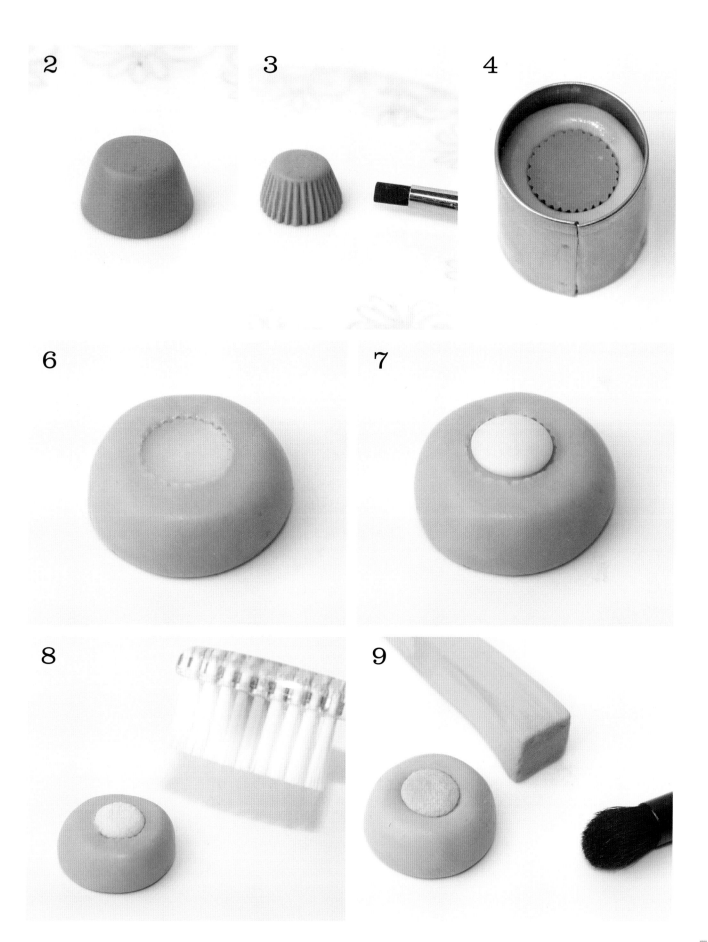

10 To make the chocolate cupcakes, I also used two variations of the same colour. For the top of the cupcakes I used dark brown; to make the bases, I tinted translucent clay with a small amount of the same colour.

11 Fill in the mould with the translucent colour.

12 Add the top using the dark brown clay and texture with a toothbrush. Bake.

13 To make the vanilla cupcakes look golden, take some beige acrylic paint and apply it to two-thirds of the bottom of the cupcake. Water the paint down a little before applying it, or soften the paint with a clean damp brush after applying it.

14 Mix the same beige colour with a little raw sienna or burnt sienna and apply below the first colour, say the bottom half of the cupcake. I like to start painting the bottom of the cupcake so that it looks cooked too.

15 Take a tiny amount of warm brown paint and brush it on the bottom edge of the cupcake, blending it with the second colour. Paint the bottom of the cupcake too.

16 Take the second caramel colour, mix it with a little water and pick up a small amount. Apply it around the edge of the cupcake and blend it so no harsh lines are visible. Note: Cupcakes bake in different ways, so you can apply this colour on top and/or in a more uneven way too.

17 Take some white acrylic paint and load the brush with it. Brush the excess away so that the bristles are flat but still have enough paint and apply it to the high points of the liner to highlight them. Keep the brush horizontal and not pointing towards the creases to avoid getting paint in the grooves. You can apply the colour around the top edge of the liner and blend it downwards with the brush or with your finger or apply it all over the ridges for more highlights.

10

14

18 To colour the chocolate cupcakes, apply a dark brown to the bottom edge to create some depth, blending it upwards, and apply white to create the highlights. Once the paint has dried, you can ice the cupcakes using whichever method described in this book you prefer (see page 22).

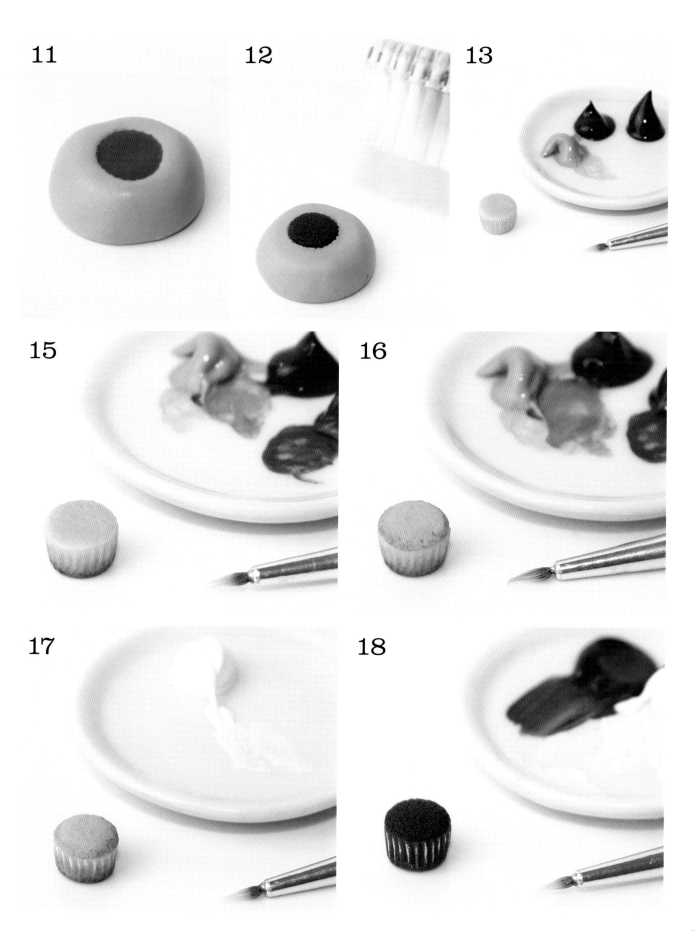

Marbled Bundt Cake and Cake Tin

IN THIS PROJECT I'LL SHOW YOU HOW TO SCULPT A BUNDT CAKE AND TIN USING A MOULD THAT YOU CAN USE AFTERWARDS TO MAKE AS MANY CAKES AS YOU LIKE. THE MOULD IS OPTIONAL: YOU COULD SCULPT THE CAKE BY ITSELF SIMPLY USING THE MARBLED CLAY.

YOU WILL NEED

- Polymer clay in dark brown and vanilla (you could use the Victoria sponge cake mix, page 36), black and scrap clay

- Talcum powder

- Silver alcohol ink

- Soft pastels in browns and white

- Acrylic paints in black, dark caramel, brown and white

- Matte or gloss varnish

- Small paintbrushes

- Ball tools

- Clay extruder

- Silicone tapered tool

- Silicone flat chisel tool

- Silicone mould putty

- Blades

- Sandpaper or nail file

- Needle tool

- Toothbrush

- Toothpick or dotting tool (optional)

- Detail tool

- Soft brush

- Fan brush

1 Take enough scrap clay to make your cake, roll it into a ball and flatten it to the desired height.

2 Use your fingers to shape the sides at an angle.

3 Take a small brush handle and push it into the centre of the cake.

4 Take a slightly larger brush and push the handle through the hole. Turn the cake over and do the same from the other side.

5 Use a large ball tool to round up the top and make the dip more natural-looking.

6 Push some more scrap clay through a clay extruder using a spaghetti setting.

7 Cut the strands of clay in half and roll one end of the strand into a point. Place the strand on the cake with the pointy end in the hollow; a silicone tapered tool might be useful here.

8 Repeat with the other strands. You can add as few or as many as you like, and make the pattern as intricate as you want. Bundt cake tins come in many different shapes and sizes; if you want to make a simple one that is even all around, you can use a toothpick and/or a dotting tool.

9 Trim the ends off and gently press the strands into the cake to secure them in place.

10 Using a small silicone flat chisel tool, catch the edge of a strand and push it down at a 45-degree angle. Do the same on the other side of the strand to create a ridge.

11 Once you've shaped all the strands, go back in with the same tool, applying a bit more pressure to define the lines and smooth down the corners.

12 Use a dotting tool or a toothpick to secure the strands inside the hollow. Bake (see page 13).

1

4

7

10
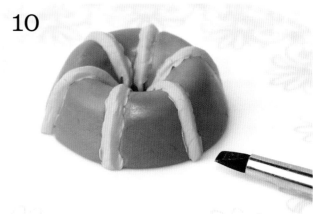

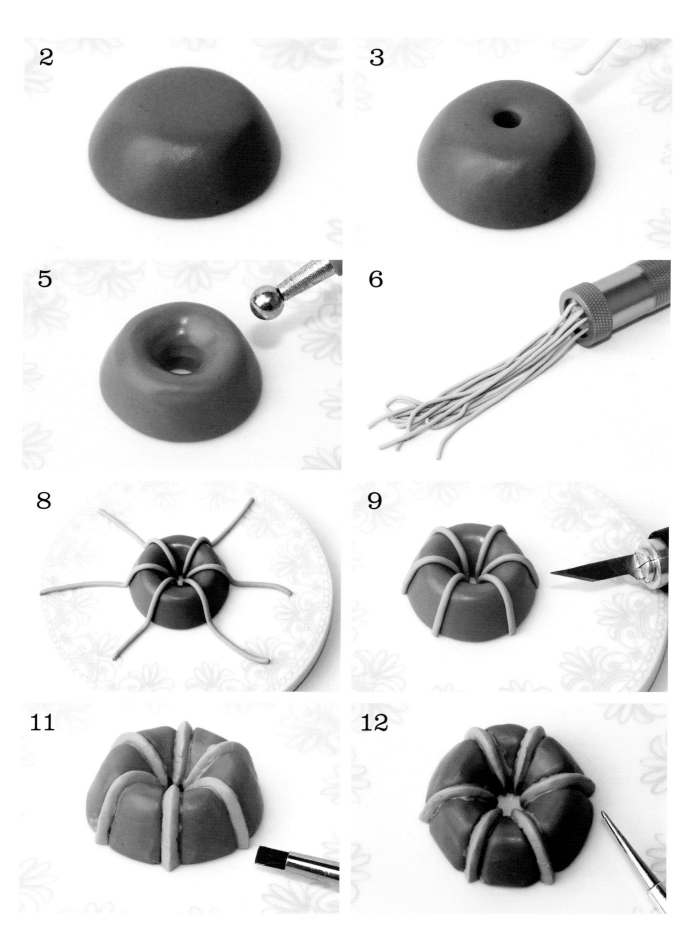

MARBLED BUNDT CAKE AND CAKE TIN 63

13 Make a mould of the cake as described on page 27 and allow to set. This way you can use the mould to create tins or more cakes in whichever flavour you like. You can even use it as a starting point to further alter the shape of the cake.

14 Place a coiled cylinder of black clay in the mould, pressing down with your fingers to secure in place.

15 Use a ball tool to push the clay in the centre first, gradually pushing the clay outwards to cover the sides and the centre of the mould.

16 Use a sharp blade to remove the excess clay. Keep thinning the clay out if needed.

17 Dust some talcum powder on the black clay and on the cake. Make sure all the ridges match up, and gently push the cake into the mould to define the inside of the tin.

18 Remove the cake and bake the tin in the mould for 30 minutes.

19 Once the cake tin is baked and cool, remove it from the mould and sand the edges or any imperfections. I use a wet nail file or sandpaper to do this because you can dip it in water, making it easier to keep clean. I like a few scratches on the base of a piece like this because it makes it look worn, but to avoid getting scratches on the clay you can use fine-grit sandpaper instead. Once you're done, wipe the tin clean.

20 Brush some silver alcohol ink on the tin to make it look metallic and let it dry completely.

21 Once the alcohol ink is dry, take some black acrylic paint mixed with a little water and apply it generously on the tin. Use a tissue to blot the excess. This will make the tin look worn and vintage-style. Let it dry and then glaze it.

Tip The technique shown in steps 22–6 works for creating the effect of marbled chocolate too.

13

17
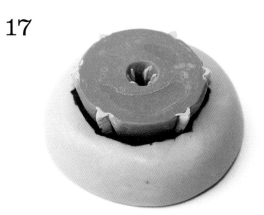

20

22 To make the cake, roll out a length of vanilla polymer clay and a slightly smaller one of dark brown.

23 Press them together and roll them a little longer so you can twist them together.

24 Fold the clay in half and twist together again.

14 15 16

18 19

21 22

23 24

MARBLED BUNDT CAKE AND CAKE TIN

25 Stretch the cylinder again, fold and twist. You can repeat this as many times as you want; however, the more you twist the less the marble effect will be. Two or three times is probably enough.

26 Now you need to make the cylinder smaller so it fits in the mould. We are used to rolling the clay outwards to stretch it, but now we need to roll it towards the centre to make it shorter.

27 Gently press and roll the ends of the clay, bringing your hands towards the centre.

28 Now take your marbled clay and push it into the mould. Cut away any excess.

29 Press the clay firmly into the mould so that it goes into all the details you created. You can use your other hand to support the wall of the mould when you push the clay.

30 Gently remove the cake from the mould and place it on an oven-proof dish. Add some general texture with a toothbrush.

31 These cakes tend to be very compact as they need to hold that beautiful shape; to add more detail, I use a soft pointy tool to create tiny holes here and there.

32 At this point, you can brown the cake with soft pastels (see page 19) or you can use acrylic paints after baking it.

33 Cut out a piece to reveal the inside.

34 Texture the sponge with a needle tool and bake.

35 Once the cake is completely cool, apply dark caramel or brown acrylic paint mixed with a little water and let dry completely.

36 Apply one coat of glaze and use a fan brush to sprinkle white soft pastels over the cake to create the illusion of icing sugar. Let it dry.

25

28

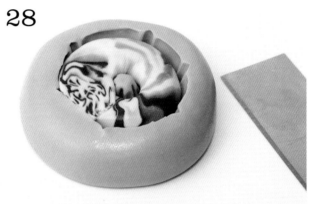

31

34

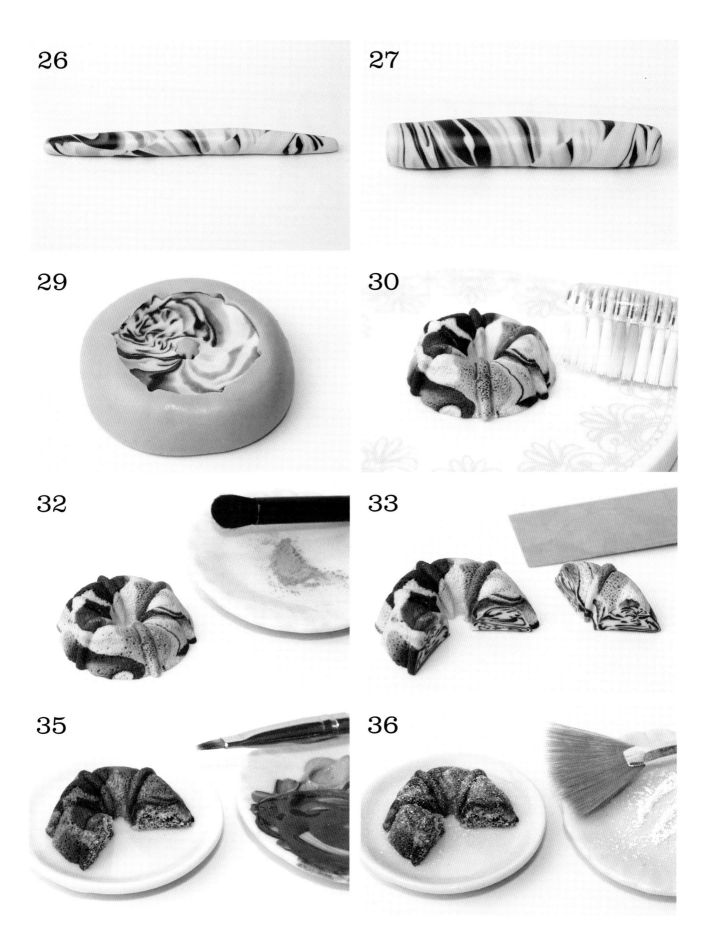

Lemon Drizzle Cake

A ZESTY LEMON DRIZZLE CAKE IS ONE OF MY FAVOURITES – BOTH AT TEATIME AND TO MAKE IN MINIATURE! I USED TINY FLOWERS TO DECORATE THE LOAF, BUT ARRANGING LEMON SLICES ON THE CAKE WILL LOOK SCRUMPTIOUS TOO. YOU CAN USE THE LEMON CANE TECHNIQUE TO MAKE SIMILAR FRUITS SUCH AS ORANGES, GRAPEFRUITS OR LIMES BY ADJUSTING THE COLOURS.

YOU WILL NEED

- For the cake: polymer clay in Victoria sponge cake mix (see page 36), light brown, yellow, translucent light brown (I used Premo in Raw Sienna) and white

- For the lemon cane: polymer clay in translucent and yellow mixed together (ratio at least 2:1), white and yellow

- Liquid polymer clay (I used FIMO Liquid)

- Acrylic paints in browns

- Lemon fragrance (optional)

- Miniature flowers

- Gloss varnish

- Rolling pin

- Craft knife/blade

- Wooden coffee stirrers

- Toothbrush

- Needle tool

- Dotting tool

- Toothpick

- Tweezers

- Silicone mould putty

- Small paintbrushes

- Mini grater

- Sandpaper

- Miniature board

1 Starting from the Victoria sponge mix, add a little light brown and more yellow polymer clay to make the sponge look a little more intense.

2 Roll out three or four thick sheets of clay, stack them together and cut out a 1 x ⅜in (2.5 x 1cm) rectangle.

3 Wrap the rectangle in a thin sheet of translucent light brown.

4 Remove the excess clay with a blade.

5 Cover the front and back as well, blending the joints with your fingers.

6 Use a craft knife to remove any excess clay from the corners.

7 Place your loaf in between two wooden coffee stirrers and press them into the clay to create the illusion of where the sponge sat in the baking tin.

8 Use a toothbrush to add general texture. You can wiggle the end of the toothbrush wherever you want to create deeper and more detailed texture.

9 Carefully remove pieces of the top of the loaf where it would have naturally torn while baking to expose the inside of the sponge.

10 Use a needle tool to texture the sponge and the crust.

11 Add little pieces of the same colour as the crust wherever you want to make the crust thicker. Blend it to the clay underneath using a dotting tool and add texture with a toothbrush.

12 Once you've added general texture, snap a toothpick in half and use the jagged end to create more details. This allows you to create grooves while texturing at the same time.

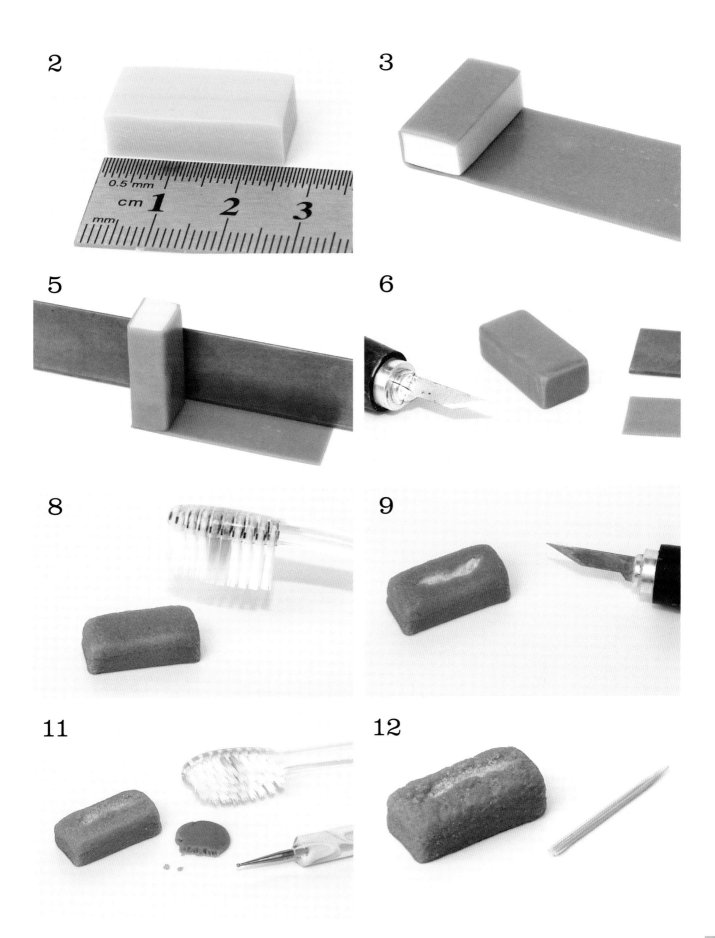

2

3

5

6

8

9

11

12

13 Dab a little liquid polymer clay on a miniature dish to stick the loaf down and cut a few slices.

14 Texture the sponge with a needle tool and arrange the slices, securing them with a little liquid polymer clay. Part-bake for 15 minutes (see page 13).

15 Once cool, use acrylic paints in warm brown tones to shade the crust a little more, starting from the lightest shades and finishing with the darkest. Let it dry completely.

16 Make some white icing (see page 22) and spread it on the loaf, using a dotting tool to drag some of it down. Add a couple of drops of lemon fragrance if you like (see page 26); don't forget to apply icing on the slices as well.

17 Grate a little pre-baked yellow clay and sprinkle it on the icing to create the illusion of lemon zest. For an extra delicate touch, I added some miniature purple flowers.

18 To make the lemon cane, start by rolling a ball of translucent yellow into a cylinder and flatten it so that it looks like a truckle of cheese.

19 Cut the cylinder in half with a sharp blade.

20 Place a thin strip of white clay in between the two halves and cut off any excess.

21 Cut the cane in half horizontally and add another strip of white clay to make a cross.

22 Repeat with another two strips to make eight sections.

23 Wrap the cane in a sheet of white clay. You can make this sheet as thick as you want, as this part of the lemon varies from one type to another.

24 Press the sheet onto the cane and roll it a few times to secure it in place.

13

16

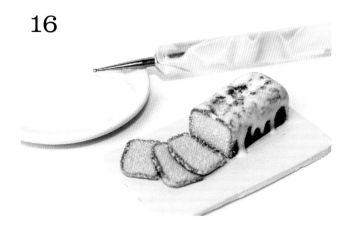

19

22

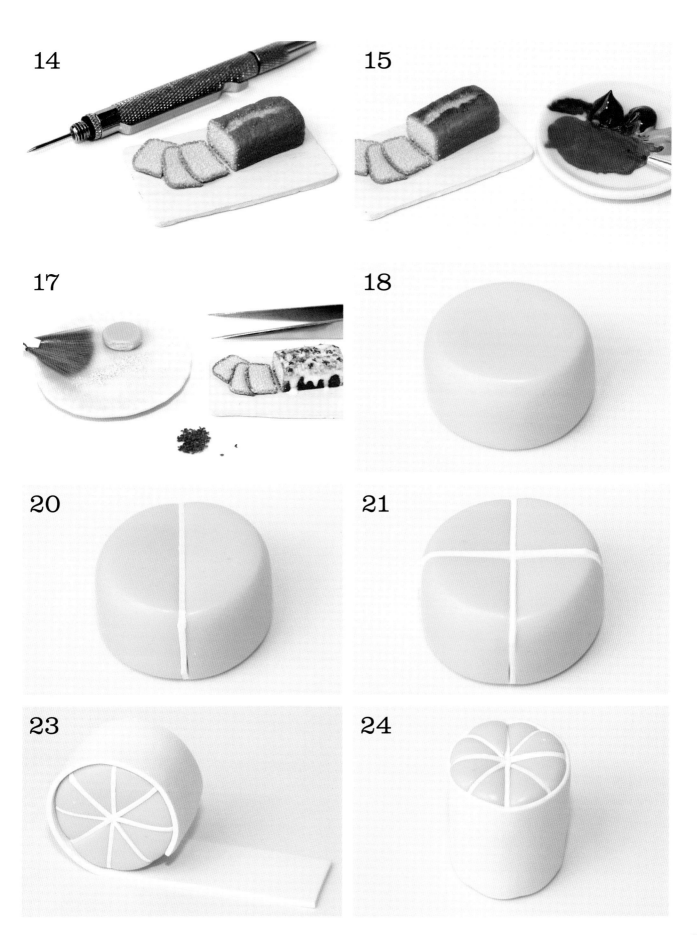

25 Wrap a sheet of yellow clay around the cane.

26 Don't start rolling the cane straight away. Secure the clay to the cane by gently pressing it and squeezing the cane from the centre out. This way you can make sure the pattern inside runs all the way through the cane.

27 Gently start rolling and stretching the cane. Keep checking the ends of the cane to make sure you can see all parts of the cane. You can trim the cane until you find the whole pattern again if necessary, or you'll need to start over.

28 Stop when you obtain the desired size. Let the cane cool down a little before slicing to prevent the colours smudging into one another.

29 Use a needle tool to texture the inside of the segments. Bake.

30 To make whole lemons, take some more yellow clay, roll it into a ball and pinch the ends.

31 Roll the ball on sandpaper to texture it.

32 If you want to create half lemons, make a lemon as in step 31 and cut it in half. Then add texture to the halves with a toothbrush and a dotting tool on the flatter end.

33 Part-bake the lemons for 15 minutes. Take some silicone mould putty and make a mould of the lemon halves (see page 27).

34 Cut a piece of the cane and pinch the ends to close them. Shape it into a lemon as in step 30 and cut it in half. Place the halves in the mould and texture with a needle tool. Bake.

35 Glue the lemons and other accessories to the board. Glaze and allow to dry.

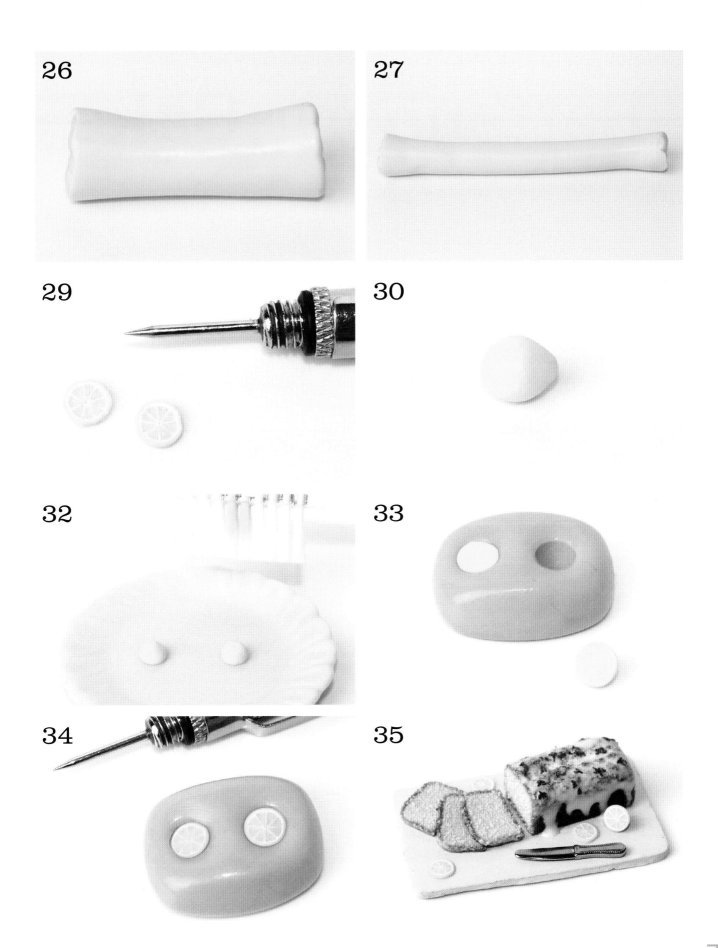

26

27

29

30

32

33

34

35

Battenberg Cake

IN THIS PROJECT WE'LL BE MAKING A SIMPLE CHECKED CANE AND TRANSFORMING IT INTO THE DAINTY CAKE THAT IS THE BATTENBERG – THE PERFECT ADDITION TO ANY MINIATURE TEA PARTY. DON'T BE AFRAID TO EXPERIMENT WITH DIFFERENT FLAVOURS OR TRY THE TECHNIQUE DESCRIBED IN THE MERMAID SCALES CAKE (SEE PAGE 118) TO TURN THIS INTO A ROUND CAKE.

YOU WILL NEED

- Polymer clay in translucent, pink, light yellow, light brown (I used Premo in Raw Sienna) and translucent red

- Liquid polymer clay (I used FIMO Liquid)

- Miniature plate, fork, knife and cake board

- Matte varnish

- Gloss varnish (optional)

- Soft pastels in white

- Pasta machine or rolling pin

- Blades

- Needle tool

- Small paintbrush

- Cyanoacrylate glue

1 To make the sponge, mix together pink and translucent for strawberry then light yellow and translucent for vanilla (the latter can be the Victoria sponge cake mix, page 36). Roll two sheets of each through settings #1 and #4 of your pasta machine and stack them together. Cut the clay into 1in (2.5cm) long rectangles, or as long as you want your cake to be.

2 Cut the clay into strips so they look square from the front.

3 Mix translucent clay with a little light brown and put it through the thinnest setting of your pasta machine. Then cover the top and bottom of the sponge strips. This will give the cakes a baked look, although you can skip this step if you like.

4 To make the jam, roll out a thin sheet of translucent red clay and cover only one side of one strip, making sure you don't cover the light brown clay. Apricot jam is used in real Battenberg cakes, so use a more orange colour if you prefer.

5 Take another strip of clay (it doesn't matter which one) and repeat.

6 Take a vanilla and a strawberry strip and stick them together. The red clay should be in the middle and the light brown clay on the top and bottom.

7 Cover the top of one of the strips with the jam clay. At this point the red clay should look like a 'T' from the front.

8 Place the other two strips on top the other way around so that the vanilla and strawberry squares aren't on top of each other.

9 Battenberg cakes are covered in a thin layer of jam to make the marzipan stick, so wrap the cane in a thin sheet of the translucent red clay.

1

4
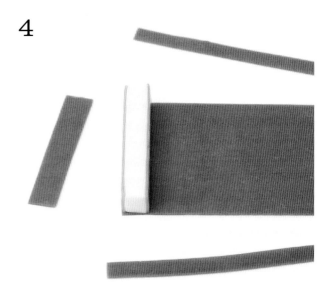

7

2

3

5

6

8

9

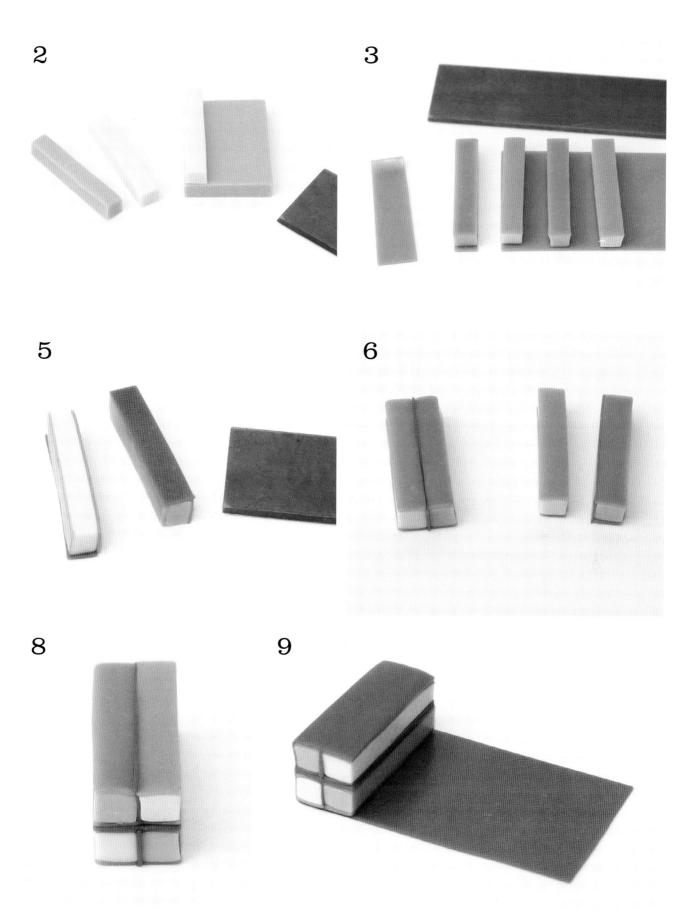

10 To make the marzipan, mix light yellow with a little light brown, then mix that with roughly two-thirds of translucent clay.

11 Roll out a sheet through setting #6 on the pasta machine and wrap the cake with it.

12 Let the cake rest for a while, then trim the ends using a sharp blade.

13 Cut out a few slices and texture the sponge with a needle tool. This cake is not very fluffy, so you can use the needle to poke a few holes here and there. Arrange the slices however you want to display them. If placed slightly overlapping each other, bond with a little liquid polymer clay.

14 Spread a little liquid polymer clay onto a miniature ceramic plate and gently press a slice on it. Texture the cake as normal. If you want the cake to look partly eaten, remove a chunk and finish texturing. Dab a little liquid polymer clay on a miniature metal fork to bond a mouthful of cake. Bake all pieces (see page 13).

15 Once baked and cool, apply a thin coat of matte varnish to the marzipan. Quickly, before it dries, stipple some white soft pastels to make it look like icing-sugar residue. You can use your finger to gently pat the pastels on too.

16 To finish, glue the cake, slices and a metal knife to a miniature board and the fork to the plate. I make the boards myself from wooden lolly sticks, but if you want to display the cake on a ceramic board instead, you can either glue it or bond it with liquid polymer clay before baking it. You can stipple a little gloss varnish on the sponges to make them look extra moist.

10

13

11

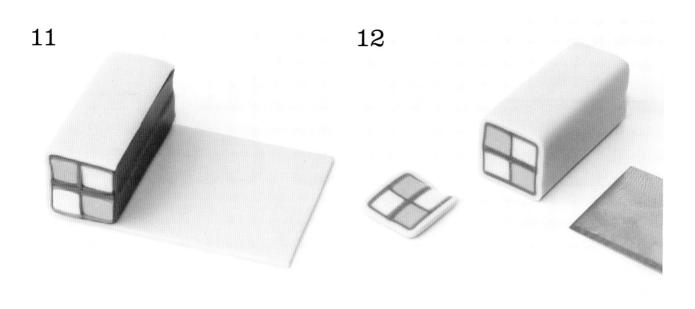

12

14

15

16

Swedish Princess Cake

ORIGINALLY CALLED 'GREEN CAKE', THIS RECIPE WAS FIRST PUBLISHED IN THE 1940S BY JENNY ÅKERSTRÖM, TEACHER TO THE DAUGHTERS OF PRINCE CARL OF SWEDEN. THE PRINCESSES LOVED THE CAKE SO MUCH THAT IT BECAME KNOWN AS SWEDISH PRINCESS CAKE. LAYERS OF AIRY SPONGE, JAM, PASTRY CREAM, WHIPPED CREAM, MARZIPAN AND ROSE DECORATIONS MAKE THIS CAKE A FEAST FOR THE EYES, EVEN IN MINIATURE.

YOU WILL NEED

- Polymer clay in Victoria sponge cake mix (see page 36) mixed with a little light brown (I used Premo in Raw Sienna) for the sponge; translucent dark red for the jam; pale yellow mixed with a little translucent for the pastry cream; and white, pink and leaf green

- Talcum powder

- Liquid polymer clay (I used FIMO Liquid)

- Acrylic paint in white

- Pasta machine or rolling pin

- Miniature plate (optional)

- Round cutter

- Blades

- Scissors (optional)

- Needle tool

- Toothpick

- Toothbrush

- Stiff-bristled paintbrush

- Detail tool

1 Roll out a sheet of sponge mix through setting #2 or #3 of your pasta machine and cut out two circles. Cut out one circle of pastry cream mix (#5). Cut out one circle of translucent dark red (#8/#9).

2 Stack the layers together starting with the sponge, then the jam, the pastry cream and another layer of sponge.

3 To make the whipped cream, take some white clay, roll it into a ball and shape it into a dome. Place it on the cake and gently press it down to secure it.

4 Roll out a sheet of sponge mix clay a little thinner than before. Cover the cake with it as described on page 24.

5 To make the thin layer of whipped cream covering the whole cake (the crumb coat), cover the cake in a very thin sheet of white clay (setting #9 on your pasta machine).

6 Finally, roll out a thin sheet of pink clay or any colour you like to make the marzipan and carefully wrap the cake with it.

7 Dust talcum powder on the cake. This will give the marzipan a matte look and create the illusion of icing sugar.

8 Use your finger to gently tap the talcum powder onto the cake, then blow away the excess.

9 Let the cake cool down a little if necessary and cut out a couple of slices.

1
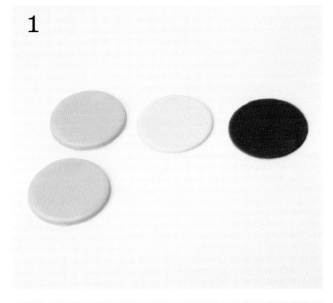

4

7

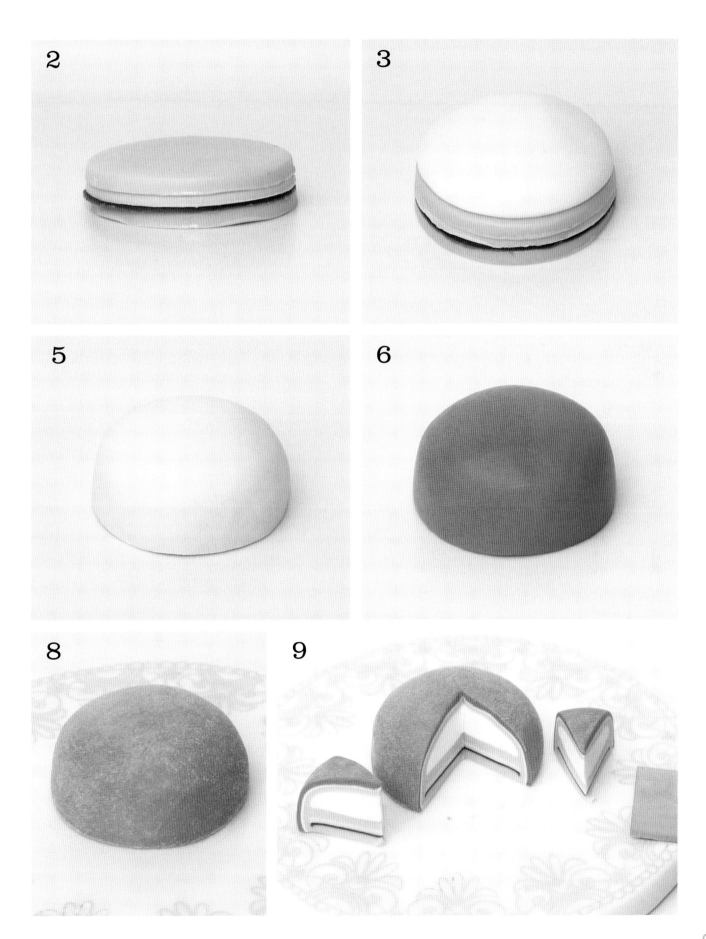

10 Use a needle tool to fluff up the sponge, teasing the jam and whipped cream a little. To texture the dome of whipped cream, use the jagged end of a toothpick. Use a needle tool to create tiny holes in the whipped cream and lines going down that a knife would have left behind, blending it into the sponge a little.

Tip Practise texturing the cream on a separate piece of clay first to see what sort of pattern the toothpick will make. Keep rotating the toothpick to avoid getting a stamp-like pattern on the clay.

11 To texture a free-standing slice, poke the whipped cream from the front as well to texture it all around, not just from the sides. If you want to display the piece on a plate, texture it first and then place it on a dish, bonding with a little liquid polymer clay.

12 If you want to make a slice lying on its side, dab a little liquid polymer clay on a miniature dish and gently press the cake on it. Texture the bottom of the cake with a toothbrush. To make the cake look part consumed, use a cutter or a knife to remove chunks of cake.

13 Texture the cake the same way as before and use a needle tool to drag some of the whipped cream away from the cake. Part-bake the cake for 15 minutes and the slices for 30 (see page 13).

14 To make the rose, roll out a thin strand of pink clay and cut out lots of pieces to make the petals. It doesn't matter if they are different sizes; you will need a variety.

15 Roll the pieces into balls and flatten them, paying attention to the edges as they tend to be very thin and delicate on a real rose.

10

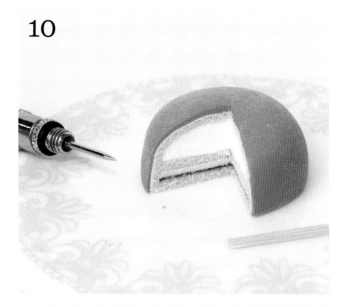

13

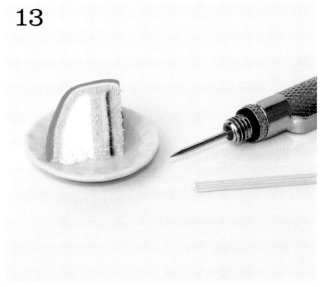

16 Take a small piece of clay and roll it into itself between your fingers or on your worktop. This is the core of the rose.

17 Take a small petal and press the bottom edge to the core of the rose, then use your fingers to pinch the top edge slightly and create those curls typical of a rose petal.

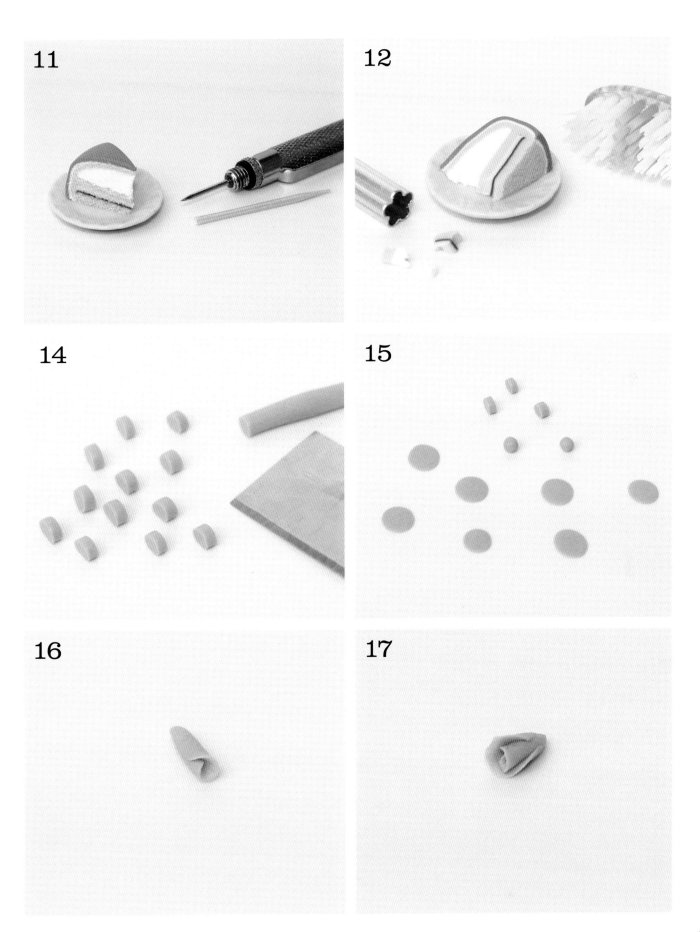

11

12

14

15

16

17

18 Add a second petal, slightly overlapping it with the first one. Use your fingers or fingernails to pinch and shape the edge of the petal.

19 Keep adding petals all around, using marginally bigger ones as you go and overlapping them slightly with the previous ones.

20 Once you're happy with your rose, gently squeeze it to secure all the petals in place and use small scissors or a blade to trim the excess clay.

21 Roll some leaf green clay into a thin strand and cut three or four pieces. Roll them into balls, then teardrops and flatten them. Use a detail tool to create the veins on the leaves and a toothbrush for a little texture. Pick them up by sliding a blade underneath and pinch the ends to make them more pointy.

22 Once the cake is cool, use a brush with stiff bristles to stipple a little white acrylic paint on it to create the illusion of icing sugar. Do the same on the slices and let dry completely.

23 Dab a little liquid polymer clay on the centre of the cake and place your leaves.

24 Pick up the rose by pushing a toothpick gently into the core, place it on the centre of the cake, and release it by rotating the toothpick on the way out. Part-bake for 10–15 minutes.

25 Once cool, cut thin triangular pieces of leaf-green clay to make the sepals (the green parts that enclose the flower bud) and attach them underneath the rose with a little liquid polymer clay. Bake for 30 minutes.

18

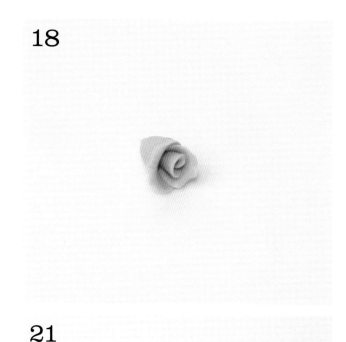

21

24

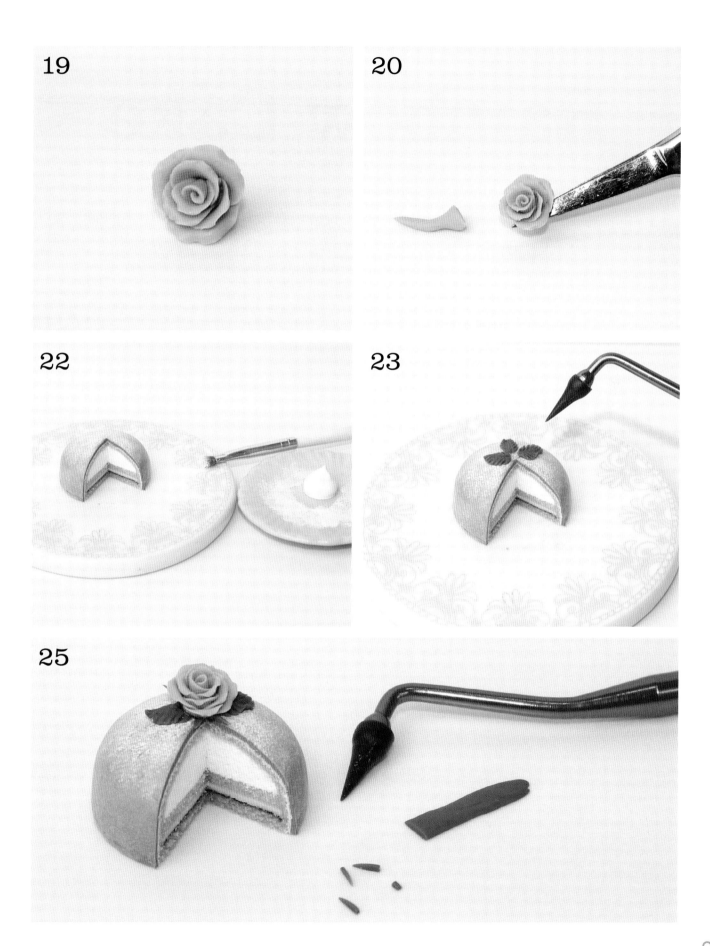

Rainbow Cake

IF YOU LIKE MODERN, MAGICAL CAKES AND PASTEL COLOURS, THIS IS THE MINIATURE FOR YOU. IN THIS PROJECT WE'LL BE USING GLITTER AND MICA POWDERS TO CREATE SUBTLE EFFECTS THAT WILL GIVE THE CAKE JUST THE RIGHT AMOUNT OF ENCHANTMENT.

YOU WILL NEED

- Polymer clays in pastel purple, pink, orange, yellow, green and light blue, and white

- White glitter dust

- White mica powder (or eyeshadow)

- Gloss varnish

- Nail caviar (optional)

- Pasta machine or rolling pin

- Round cutter

- Blades

- Needle tool

- Angle chisel

- Plastic card, such as an old loyalty card

- Baking parchment

- Toothpick

- Tape

- Dotting tool

- Detail tool

- Fan brush

- Small paintbrush

1 To make the rainbow layers of sponge, you'll need polymer clay in pastel colours. FIMO has a pastel range, but you can make your own by simply mixing your chosen colours with white. I mixed some translucent clay with the colours so that they weren't completely opaque and rolled out sheets through setting #1 of my pasta machine, then cut out a circle of each colour (six in total).

2 Roll out a thin sheet of white polymer clay (setting #6/7) and cut out five circles. Stack the layers in order starting from any colour you like, adding a layer of white clay in between the colours.

3 Cut out a couple of slices to reveal the inside and texture the sponge with a needle tool.

4 Take the same rainbow colours, roll them into cylinders and put them through setting #3/4 of your pasta machine. Stack the layers in order and cut a few strips to make the rainbow decoration.

5 Take a strip and shape it into a rainbow on an oven-safe dish. You can initially use your hands and then an angle chisel to perfect it. If you want the rainbow to be seen from the top instead of from the front, shape it around something round and oven-safe such as a metal cutter. Part-bake (see page 13).

6 Make some white buttercream (see page 22) and cover the cake in it. To make it as smooth as you can, take a plastic card and wrap it with baking parchment, securing it with a little tape. Press the card onto the icing and quickly pull it away or the icing will come away with it.

7 Take a toothpick and run it down the sides and along the cut edge of the cake to get rid of the excess icing and to make it look as if a real knife has cut through the cake. You may need to do this a few times to achieve a neat finish.

8 Take your baked and cool rainbow decoration and push it into the icing, making sure it's straight. The icing needs to be firm to hold the decoration in place while baking. Part-bake.

1

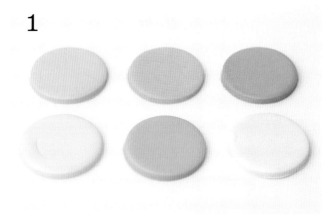

5

9 To make the drip effect, make some light blue icing and spread it on the top of the cake. Pick up some more icing with a fine dotting tool and drag it down to create the drips. Part-bake.

10 Once the cake is cool, take small beads of white clay in different sizes and place them around the base of the rainbow to make the clouds. Start from the bigger beads of clay and gradually move on to smaller ones, filling any gaps. Bake.

11 Spread some glaze on the rainbow only and quickly before it dries, sprinkle white glitter dust on it using a fan brush. Do the same on the back.

12 Mix white mica powder with a little gloss varnish and use it to paint the clouds. Glaze the sky drips and let them dry completely. Sprinkle some nail caviar before the glaze dries for extra magic if you like. Then glaze the cake again to protect the decorations.

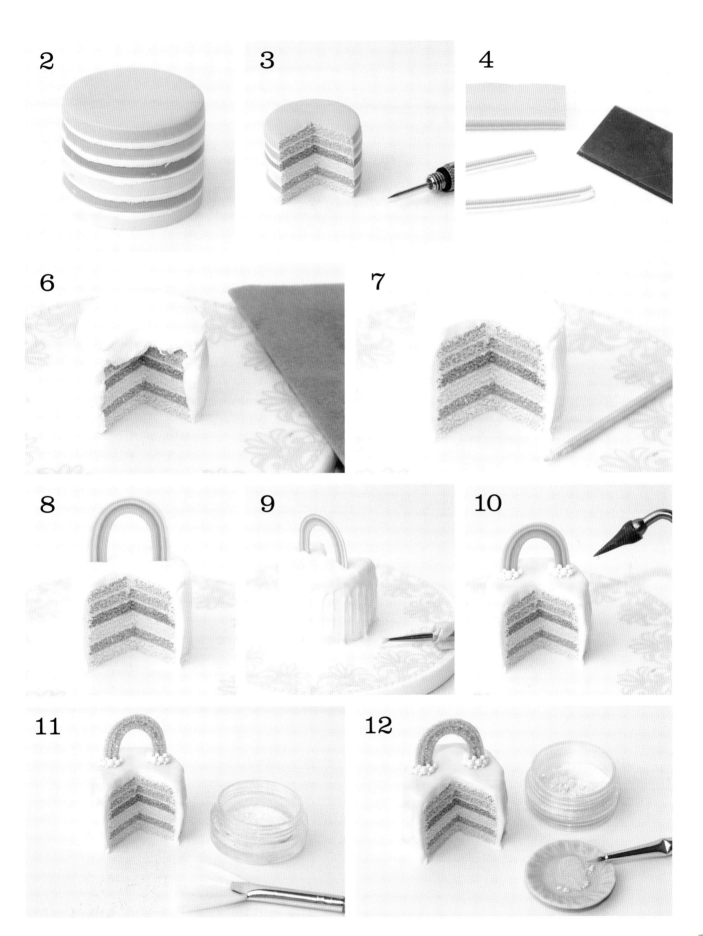

Confetti Birthday Cake

NOTHING SAYS 'BIRTHDAY' LIKE A CONFETTI CAKE. IT IS FUN, COLOURFUL AND WILL MAKE YOUR MINIATURE CAKE COLLECTION A LOT BRIGHTER. IN THIS PROJECT WE USE COLD PORCELAIN TO MAKE THE TINY BUTTERCREAM DECORATIONS; I LOVE TO PIPE DETAILS WHEN I GET THE CHANCE. YOU COULD SCULPT THE CREAM OUT OF POLYMER CLAY TOO.

YOU WILL NEED

- Polymer clay in Victoria sponge cake mix (see page 36), pink, white and pastel blue

- Liquid polymer clay (I used FIMO Liquid)

- Acrylic paints in confetti colours of your choice

- Cold porcelain (see page 23) in white

- Gloss varnish

- Pasta machine or rolling pin

- Round cutter

- Blades

- Needle tool

- Flat-edged tool

- Tweezers

- Toothpick

- Small paintbrush

- PVA glue

- Small open-star icing nozzle and piping bags

- Jute string

- Scissors

1   For the cake layers you will need three circles of Victoria sponge cake mix (setting #1), browned as described on page 18, and two layers of pink (setting #6/7) for the icing.

2   Stack the layers, making sure they're all straight. If any of the icing sticks out a little, trim it off.

3   Cut out a couple of slices, or more if you like.

4   Texture the inside of the sponges with a needle tool. If arranging the slices on a plate, attach them with a little liquid polymer clay.

5   To make the candles, take some white and pastel blue clay and roll it into thin, even strands.

6   Twist the strands together, keeping even pressure on the clay and gently rolling it to secure the clay in place.

7   Once the clay is secure, keep rolling and stretching it. Once you have obtained the desired thickness, part-bake (see page 13).

1

4

2

3

5

6

7

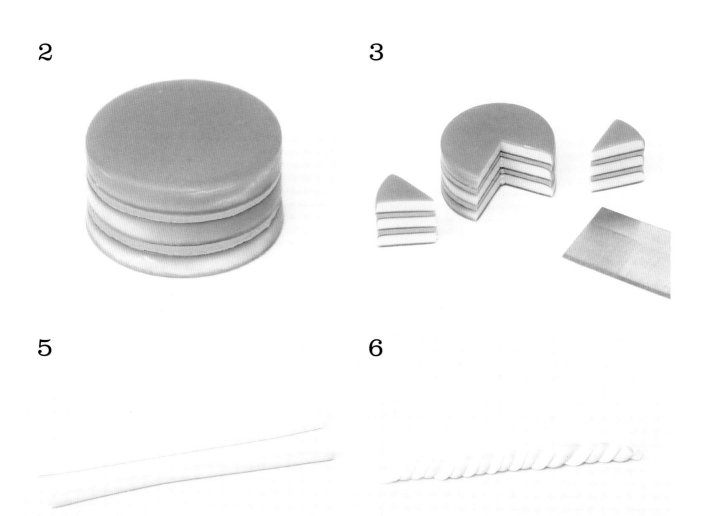

8 Once cool, chop up the clay into even pieces to make the candles.

8

9 Take some pink buttercream and cover the sides of the cake first. Use a flat-edged tool as a scraper to make the sides as neat as you can and to drag the buttercream around the top edge inwards towards the centre of the cake. Then use a toothpick to neaten up the edges as if a real knife has cut through the cake. Add icing to the slices as well. Part-bake the cake for 15 minutes and the slices for 30.

10 Cover the top of the cake with more icing and smooth it down as much as you can. Gently press the candles into the icing (they are very fragile) and bake for 30 minutes.

10

11 To create the illusion of confetti in the sponge, using a small brush, apply dots of acrylic paint in the sponge. Use a little water to dilute the colour and soak up the excess with a clean brush. I do this so that the colour goes right into the sponge rather than just sitting on the clay. If you lose some intensity, go back in with a little more paint and apply it somewhere in the middle of the confetti. You can also create a wash of the colour and apply that as well.

Tip Apply a couple of dots of paint at a time and dilute them straight away or they will dry before you get a chance to blend them.

12

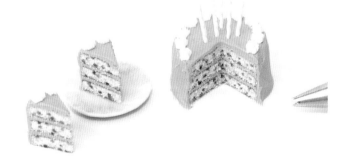

12 To make the piped decorations, apply a little PVA glue around the edge of the cake and pipe white cold porcelain (see page 23) using a small open-star icing nozzle. Let it dry completely and stipple a little glaze on the sponge.

13 To finish off the candles, take a piece of jute string, separate the strands and cut lots of small pieces just big enough for you to pick them up. Apply a tiny dot of PVA glue on top of the candles and place the strands of jute string. Once the glue has dried, trim the excess.

9

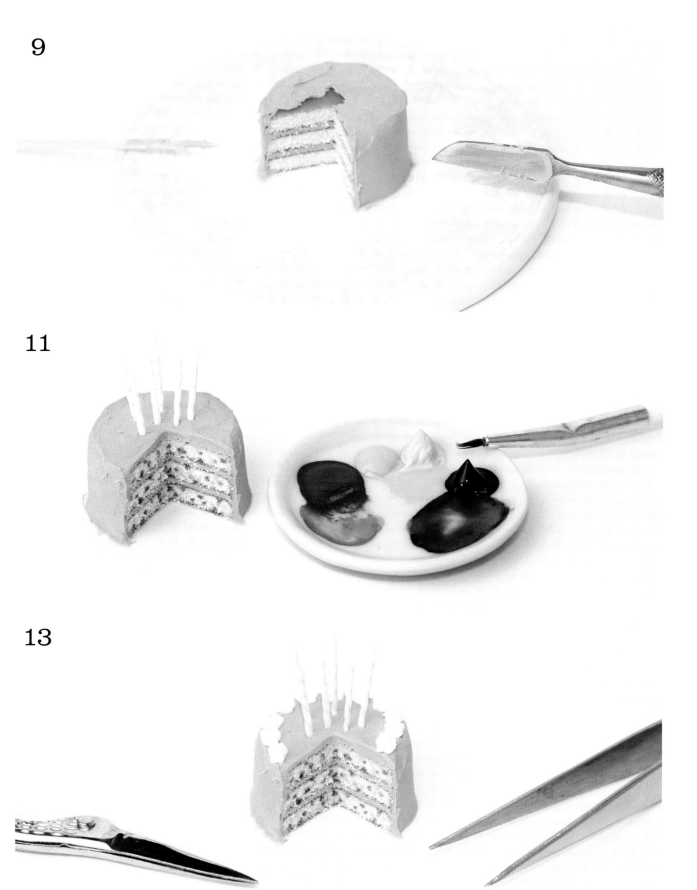

11

13

Unicorn Cake

THIS UNICORN CAKE HAS PASTEL PINK ICING AND PIPED DECORATIONS, BUT YOU COULD CHOOSE A MORE TRADITIONAL WHITE BUTTERCREAM AND DECORATE IT HOWEVER YOU LIKE. MAKE THE MANE ENTIRELY OUT OF SPRINKLES, FLOWERS OR FRUIT, OR ADD A DOUGHNUT OR MACARON – LET YOUR IMAGINATION RUN WILD.

YOU WILL NEED

- Polymer clay in pastel pink, purple, mint (I used FIMO Effect), pastel yellow, white, black and scrap clay

- Liquid polymer clay (I used FIMO Liquid)

- Nail caviar

- Gold mica powder (or eyeshadow)

- Gloss varnish

- Pasta machine or rolling pin

- ¾in (2cm) round cutter

- Flat tool

- Soft brush

- Silicone tapered sculpting tool

- Tweezers

- Small paintbrush

- Dotting tool

- Detail tool

1 Put some scrap clay through the thickest setting of your pasta machine and cut out six circles using a ¾in (2cm) round cutter. Stack the circles together and part-bake (see page 13), bonding them to a sculpting base with a little liquid polymer clay. This will allow the cake to stay put when you add the icing.

2 Once baked and cool, cover the cake in pastel pink (or white) buttercream mix (see page 22), making it as smooth as you can with a flat tool.

3 Use some gold nail caviar to decorate the bottom edge of the cake.

Tip Dip the dotting tool in a tiny bit of liquid polymer clay to pick up the nail caviar.

4 To make the unicorn horn, roll out two elongated teardrops of white clay.

5 Twist them together. Once secure, you can either roll them gently on your work surface to stretch the horn and make it thinner or keep twisting it between your fingers as you stretch it, whichever feels more natural to you.

6 Trim the horn if necessary and dust it with gold mica powder (or eyeshadow) using a soft brush to give it a beautiful metallic shine (use another colour if you prefer).

7 To make the ears, roll two small balls of clay into teardrops and flatten them slightly.

8 Use a soft silicone tool with a tapered point to shape the ears. Part-bake the horn and ears for 10 minutes.

9 Once baked and cool, push the horn and ears into the buttercream and part-bake.

Tip The buttercream needs to be firm for it to hold up the horn and ears while baking.

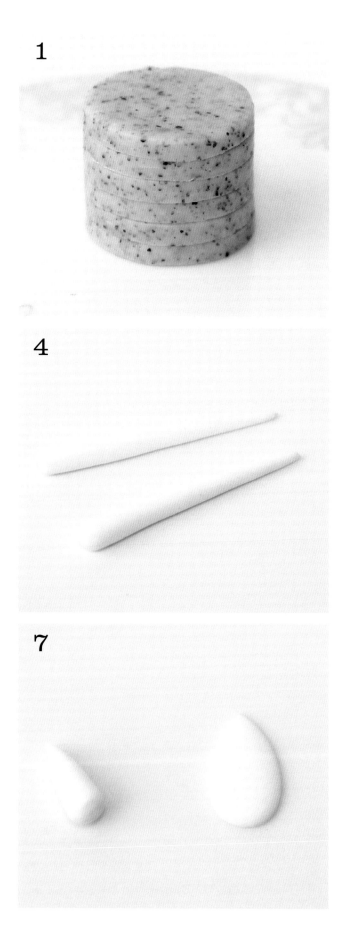

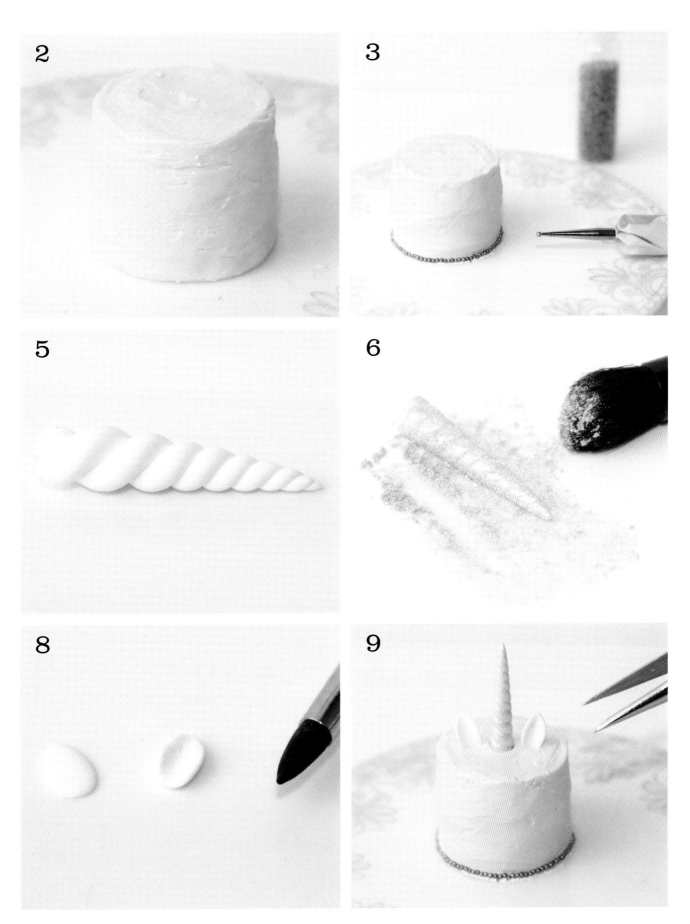

10 Once the cake is out of the oven and cool, mix some gloss varnish with the same mica powder used for the horn and paint the inside of the ears.

11 Brush a little liquid polymer clay on the part of the cake where you want the eyes to be and cut tiny pieces of black clay. Roll the pieces into thin strands and place the main eyeline first. Give it a little push so that it stays on the cake while you give it the final shape with a soft tapered tool. Once the main eyeline is in place, add another two small lashes on the ends and part-bake.

12 To make the rosette-like decorations, roll some purple clay into a strand and cut lots of small, even pieces. Roll them into balls, flatten them slightly and use a small dotting tool to trace a spiral on the clay. Then use the same dotting tool to soften the line and create a deeper groove.

13 To make the meringue kisses, roll pastel yellow clay into tiny balls and pinch the tops as you turn them. You can also roll the balls into teardrops with fine tops and then press the base down onto your work surface to flatten it.

14 To make the star-shaped decorations, roll pink clay into tiny balls and flatten them. Press a soft silicone tool with a tapered point around the sides to create the grooves and obtain the star shape.

15 To create the Sultane-style meringues or decorations, start from a small flattened ball of mint clay and poke a hole in the centre with a dotting tool. Use a fine-ended tool to trace lines from the base towards the hole. You may need to reshape the hollow again after this step.

16 Spread a thin layer of liquid polymer clay on the cake and add the decorations. Start from the front to get a neater finish, and move on to cover the top of the cake. You can draw an imaginary line (or a real one) on the cake so you have an idea of where you want the mane to be and keep the decorations within those lines. Bake one last time.

10

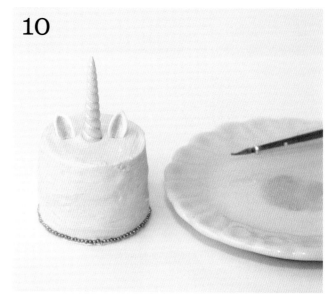

13

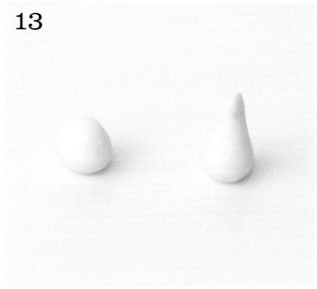

17 Once cool, glaze the decorations one bit at a time. Before the glaze dries, fill in any gaps with different-coloured nail caviar or sprinkles. I filled in the Sultane meringues with pink nail caviar, which I think looks really cute. Once the glaze is dry, glaze it again to add an extra layer of protection on the decorations and glaze the horn and ears.

Melted Ice-Cream Cone Cake

IF YOU LIKE BOTH ICE CREAM AND CAKE, WHY NOT COMBINE THE TWO? THIS IS SUCH A FUN CAKE TO MAKE, AND YOU COULD CHANGE THE COLOURS OF THE ICING AND THE ICE CREAM TO RECREATE YOUR FAVOURITE FLAVOURS. ADD AS FEW OR AS MANY DECORATIONS AS YOU WANT: THE POSSIBILITIES ARE INFINITE.

YOU WILL NEED

- Polymer clay in dark brown (I used Premo in Burnt Umber), lavender, beige (I used Premo in Ecru), vanilla mixed with a little translucent and white, and scrap clay

- Soft pastels in earth tones

- Liquid polymer clay (I used FIMO Liquid)

- Nail caviar

- Acrylic paint in warm brown

- Gloss and matte varnishes

- Pasta machine or rolling pin

- Round cutter

- Flat tool

- Blade

- Toothbrush

- Needle tool

- Toothpick

- Tweezers

- Small paintbrush

- Dotting tool

- Detail tool

1 Roll out a sheet of vanilla polymer clay and a sheet of scrap clay through the thickest setting of your pasta machine. Cut out one circle of vanilla and four circles of scrap clay. It doesn't matter what colour these are, as they won't be visible in the final product. Stack the circles together on an oven-proof dish starting with the vanilla layer. Part-bake (see page 13).

2 Make some lavender buttercream mix (see page 22) and use it to cover the cake. Use a flat tool to smooth down the buttercream as much as possible. Part-bake.

Tip To smooth down the top, I like to keep the flat tool in place and rotate the dish.

3 Make a doughnut following the instructions in the doughnut earrings project on page 144. Once you've added soft pastels on the top, turn it over, gently texture the base with a toothbrush and dust that with soft pastels too.

4 To make the macaron shells, mix the vanilla clay with a little white so that it looks like white chocolate. Roll out a thin strand and cut out even pieces. Roll the pieces into four balls and flatten them into a slightly domed shape. Then use a needle tool to texture the bottom edges. Part-bake the macaron shells and the doughnut.

5 Once the macaron shells are baked and cool, brush a little liquid polymer clay on the inside and press a small ball of dark brown clay into one of them. Take another shell and gently press it on the clay until you can see the chocolate reach the edges. Make the second macaron the same way.

6 Spread lavender icing on the doughnut and add a few stripes of chocolate. Part-bake the doughnuts and macarons.

1

4

7 Make an ice-cream cone following the instructions on page 176. Line the inside of the cone with liquid polymer clay and fill it with chocolate clay. Roll a separate ball to make the melted ice cream.

8 Once your cake is baked and cool, spread a little liquid polymer clay or chocolate icing (see page 22) where you want your ice cream to be and press the ball of chocolate clay on it. Then take the cone and press it onto the ice cream scoop.

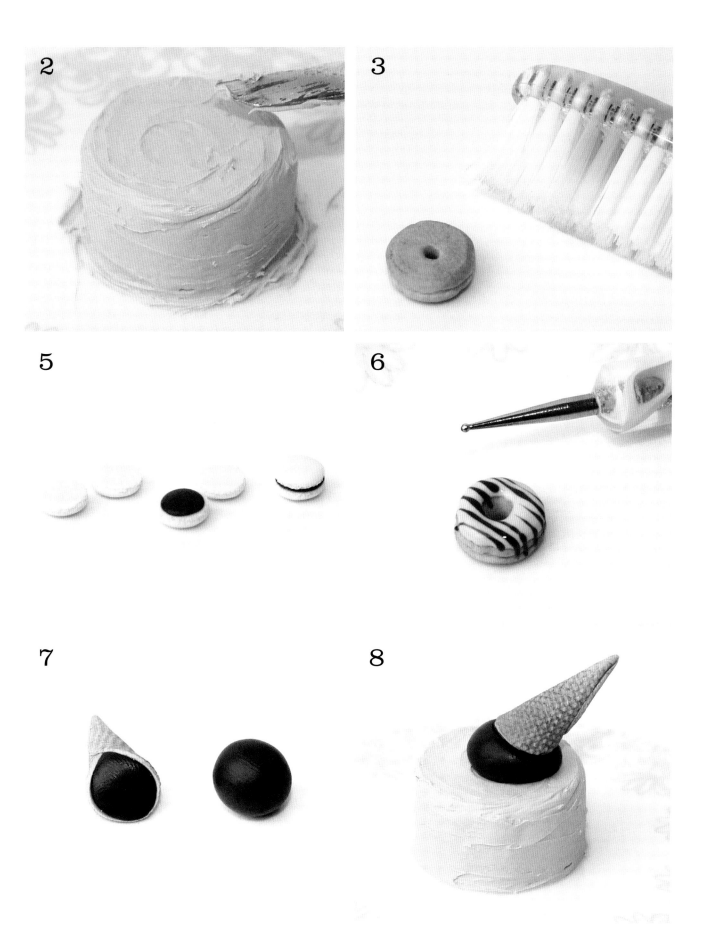

9 Add some texture to the ice cream with a toothpick and a toothbrush.

10 Use a dotting tool to spread some chocolate icing around the ice cream and only on the top of the cake at this point. Place your baked doughnut, gently pressing it into the ice cream for support.

11 Place one macaron in front of the doughnut and use a brush to dab some chocolate icing around the top edge of the cone.

12 To make the drips, mix the chocolate icing with a little more solid clay to make it stiffer. Use a small dotting tool to drag it down the cake. I like to make the drips a little thicker than icing, so that they hold more shape, appear more three-dimensional and don't run down the cake and collect at the bottom.

13 Use a dotting tool to create little 'bridges' between the drips. Then take some more chocolate mix and fill in the gaps.

14 Once you've made all the drips, place your second macaron, using the drips as glue.

15 As a final touch, add some nail caviar. I didn't sprinkle them but used tweezers to place them carefully, to prevent them from accumulating in unwanted places. Bake.

16 Add a little more colour to the cone using warm brown acrylic paint. Glaze the doughnut and chocolate drips with gloss varnish and the cone with a little matte varnish.

9

12

15

10

11

13

14

16

MELTED ICE-CREAM CONE CAKE 111

Shabby Chic Rose Bouquet Cake

I USED TO MAKE SO MANY CAKES WITH POLKA-DOT FONDANT AND FABRIC-INSPIRED ROSES THAT THIS SHABBY CHIC CREATION SOON BECAME MY SIGNATURE CAKE. HERE I WILL ALSO SHOW YOU A TECHNIQUE TO OBTAIN A VERTICAL LAYER CAKE.

YOU WILL NEED

- Polymer clay in white, red, translucent, Victoria sponge cake mix (see page 36), white for the fondant (I used Sculpey Ultra Light), pink, green and different colours to make the roses

- Liquid polymer clay (I used FIMO Liquid)

- Acrylic paint in white

- Matte glaze

- Pasta machine or rolling pin

- Blades

- Round cutter

- Needle tool

- Dotting tool

- Toothpick

- Brush

- Detail tool

1 Roll out a sheet of Victoria sponge cake mix through the thickest setting of your pasta machine and cut out a strip as wide as you would like your cake to be high. Roll out two thin sheets of clay, one of red and translucent mixed together and one of white, and stack them together. Trim the excess clay and trim the end at an angle so it is easier to roll. Make sure the sponge is on the outside when you roll the cake.

2 Trim the excess clay on the top and bottom of the cake to make it as straight as possible.

3 Trim the excess clay at an angle and blend it to the rest of the cake, trying to make the whole shape as round as possible.

4 Roll a sheet of white clay through the thinnest setting of your pasta machine and cover the sides of the cake with it.

5 Cut out a circle big enough to cover the top and blend the edges.

6 Cover the cake with fondant as described on page 24. I used a mix of Sculpey Ultra Light and pink polymer clay because this looks very similar to fondant, but you can use any clay you like.

7 Let the cake rest for a while, then cut out a couple of slices to reveal the vertical layers.

8 Texture the inside of the cake with a needle tool and part-bake (see page 13).

9 Take some polymer clay in different colours to make the roses and roll them into long thin strands.

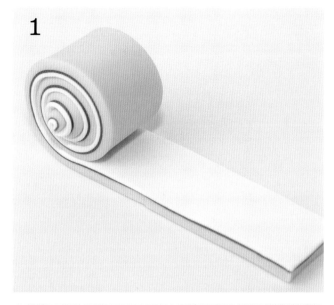

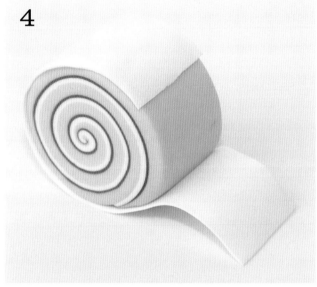

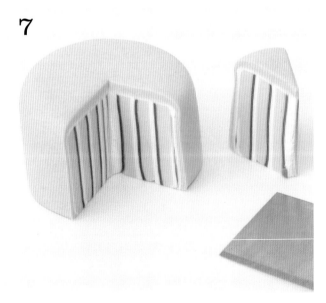

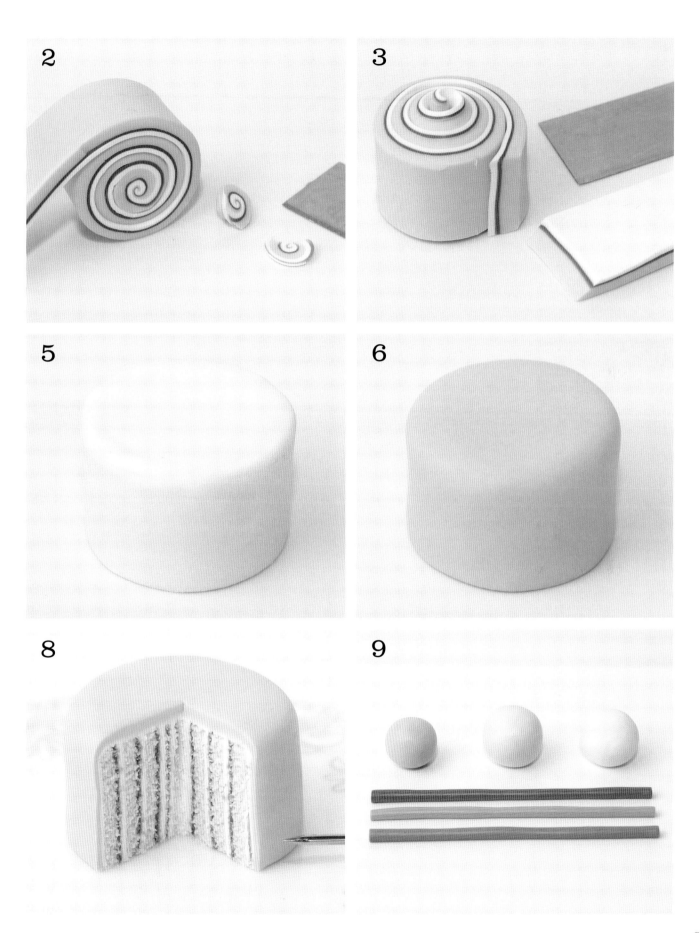

10 Put them through setting #6/7 of your pasta machine. The clay needs to be quite firm for this or you won't get the jagged edge required. If the clay is too soft, let it rest for a while.

11 To make the rose, roll the clay into itself, applying pressure at the base and not on the whole flower so that the edges remain open.

12 Gently squeeze the base of the flower and turn it, then squeeze and turn, squeeze and turn again a few times. Then gently roll it thinner.

13 Trim the flower at the base. Make some more roses in the other colours of your choice.

14 Take a ball of green clay and flatten it into a dome. Make some leaves (see page 88), then place them all around the edge of the dome.

15 Place the first rose in the middle and another two on the sides. I like to hover the first flower in the middle before securing it to the base to make sure I can add the ones on the sides without having any gaps or spaces or before I realize the base is too small.

16 Fill in the gaps with another couple of roses. You can either part-bake the bouquet before adding it to the cake and bake it all again, or you can carefully lift it off with a blade and place it on the cake, bonding with liquid polymer clay. Bake.

17 Once baked and cool, take some white acrylic paint and, using a small dotting tool, poke lots of dots on the fondant in any pattern you like. Wipe the dotting tool clean every few dots to avoid making gradually bigger dots as the paint dries. Once dry, glaze the fondant with a little matte varnish to protect the paint.

Tip If the paint is too creamy, try mixing it with a little water. Practise dotting the paint on a piece of paper first to make sure you don't have too much on the tool.

10

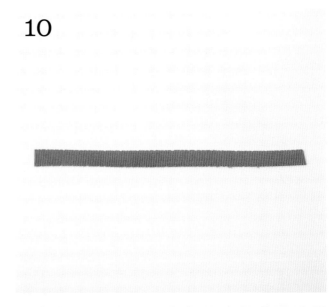

13

11

12

14

15

16

17

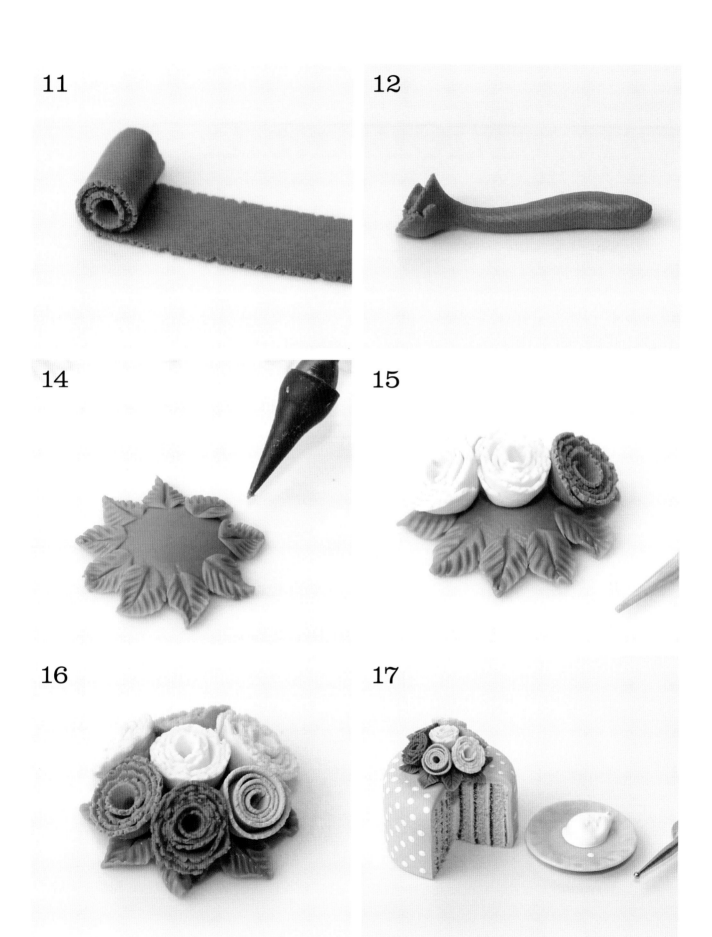

Mermaid Scales Cake

I LOVE TO SCUPLT MERMAID SCALES AND BARNACLES ON MY PIECES. IT IS MY WAY TO EXPRESS HOW I SEE THE CONNECTION BETWEEN EVERYTHING IN THIS WORLD AND HOW NONE OF OUR ACTIONS IS ISOLATED. SO, IN THIS PROJECT, I SHOW YOU HOW TO MAKE MERMAID SCALES AND BARNACLES, AND HOW TO ATTACH THEM TO POLYMER CLAY PIECES.

YOU WILL NEED

- Polymer clay in Victoria sponge cake mix (see page 36), white, translucent and yellow

- Mica powders (or eyeshadows) in colours of your choice

- Liquid polymer clay (I used FIMO Liquid)

- Acrylic paints in pink, yellow, turquoise and white

- Gloss varnish

- Pasta machine or rolling pin

- Nail caviar

- Round cutters in different sizes

- Craft knife and blades

- Needle tool

- Dotting tool

- Tapered sculpting tools, large and small

- Small paintbrushes

- Detail tool

1 Roll out a thin sheet of white polymer clay (setting #6/7 of your pasta machine) and cut out three circles to make the icing. Take a smaller cutter and cut out a circle.

2 Mix translucent clay with a small amount of yellow clay and put it through the same setting of your pasta machine. Cut out circles using the smaller cutter and fill in the hole in the white clay.

3 To make the sponge layers, use the Victoria sponge cake mix (browned if you prefer; see page 18) or any other flavour, and stack the layers together.

4 Roll out a thin strip of white clay and cover the sides of the cake with it.

5 Cut out a circle and cover the top, blending the edges with your fingers.

6 Cut out a couple of slices.

7 Texture the inside with a needle tool.

8 Make some white cream mix (see page 22), cover the cake and use a dotting tool to create swirls. Part-bake (see page 13).

9 To make the mermaid scales, roll out a strand of translucent clay and cut into small pieces. Roll the pieces into balls and flatten them. Using a needle tool, indent lines on the clay, converging towards the centre.

10 Take some mica powders (or eyeshadows) in colours you like and dust them on the scales. Part-bake.

Tip Dust the mica powders on an oven-safe dish so you don't risk damaging the scales when transferring them onto another baking tray. If you want, you can lift them to give the scales some movement.

1

5
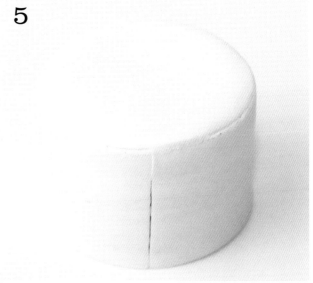

8

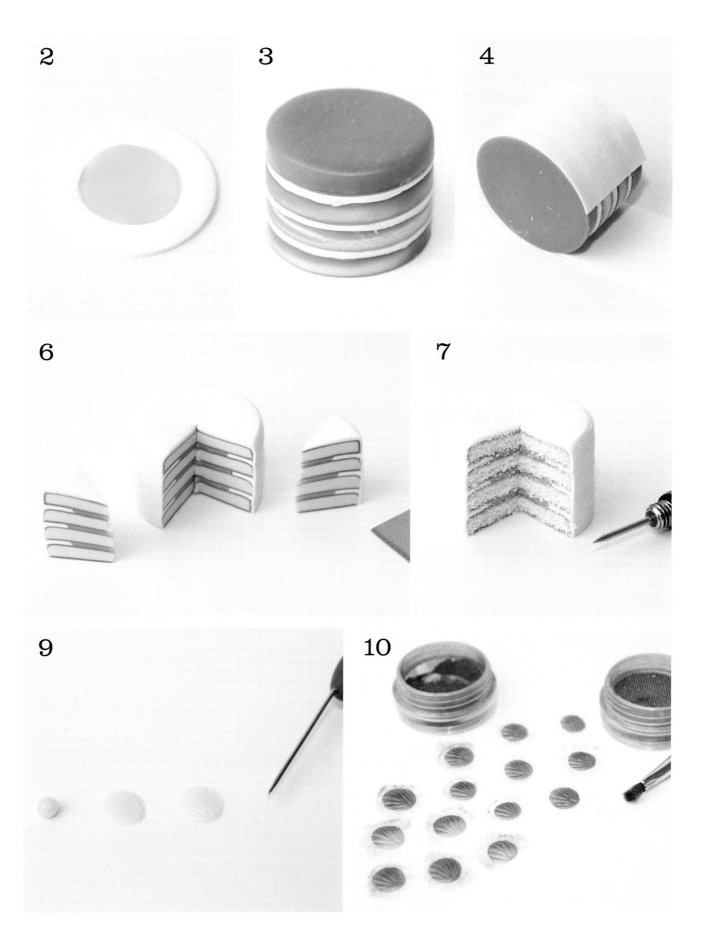

11 To make a barnacle, shape a ball of white clay into a flat cone. In the following steps I'll show you this in larger scale so you can practise the technique, but you will need to make barnacles directly on the cake.

12 Use a tapered sculpting tool to create indents, to obtain five or six sections divided by ridges, rather like a meringue.

13 Poke the clay with a dotting tool to texture it and gently push it into the peak of the barnacle to create a hole.

14 Once the cake is baked and cool, sculpt some tiny barnacles using the technique you practised in steps 11–13, but now with a much smaller sculpting tool. Once you've made a few, dip the base of the mermaid scales into some liquid polymer clay and push them into the barnacles. Trim the scales if they are too big or it you want some of them to look as if they're stuck deeper in the barnacles. Bake.

15 Take some acrylic paint in pink and paint all the barnacles, making sure the paint goes in the holes as well.

16 Add some yellow acrylic paint, leaving some pink visible.

17 Add a little turquoise. Don't be afraid to go back in with the previous colours to blend them into different colours.

18 Load your paintbrush with white paint and wipe away the excess to make the bristles flat. Gently swipe the flat brush on the ridges and highest points of the barnacles to highlight them.

19 When the paint is completely dry, spread a little glaze on the barnacles and add some nail caviar. Let the glaze dry before applying a second coat to seal in the decorations and to give the mermaid scales a beautiful shine.

Naked Wedding Cake

THIS IS THE PERFECT BEGINNERS' WEDDING CAKE, AS YOU DON'T HAVE TO WORRY ABOUT MAKING THE ICING LOOK FLAWLESS. IF YOU DON'T FEEL READY TO MAKE A THREE-TIER CAKE YET, START WITH A SINGLE ONE INSTEAD.

YOU WILL NEED

- Polymer clay in light beige, dark brown, Victoria sponge cake mix (see page 36), white, translucent, pink, orange, purple, green and scrap clay

- Soft pastels in beige and caramel

- Liquid polymer clay (I used FIMO Liquid)

- Talcum powder

- Acrylic paint in browns and white

- Gloss varnish

- Nail caviar

- Pasta machine or rolling pin

- Round cutters in a range of sizes

- Toothbrush

- Soft brush

- Toothpick

- Flat-sided soft silicone tool

- Craft knife

- Dotting tools

- Blades or scissors

- Detail tool

- Small flat brush

1 Roll out a sheet of polymer clay in a vanilla colour (Victoria sponge cake mix) through the thickest setting of your pasta machine. Cut out three sets of three circles using 1in (2.5cm), 1¼in (3cm) and 1½in (4cm) cutters, or any other size you want; what matters is that you have three distinguishable sizes with a harmonious transition between them.

2 Texture the sponges with a toothbrush, paying particular attention to the sides, as that is where the icing will sit.

3 Use a soft brush to dust the sponges with beige soft pastels all over and the edges with a darker caramel colour. Part-bake (see page 13).

4 Squeeze a little liquid polymer clay onto an oven-proof dish and place the first layer of sponge. Cut out a smaller circle of scrap clay and bond it to the sponge with a little liquid polymer clay.

5 Sandwich the rest of the sponge and scrap clay layers, bonding with liquid polymer clay. I use smaller circles in between the sponges to make room for the buttercream.

6 Stack the rest of the tiers, making sure they are straight, and part-bake. You can also assemble the tiers separately first and then stack them; however, I recommend not applying liquid polymer clay on the base of the top two tiers, as this will create an uneven surface that will make your cake wonky when assembled.

7 Once the cake is cool, make some white buttercream (see page 22) and use a toothpick or fine tool to fill the gaps, allowing some to stick out. Turning the toothpick will help you release the clay into the cake.

8 Use a soft silicone tool (or toothpick for a more rustic look) with a flat side to scrape away and smooth down all the buttercream. If there are any gaps left, go back in with more buttercream and repeat. Cover the rest of the cake with a thin layer of buttercream and part-bake.

1

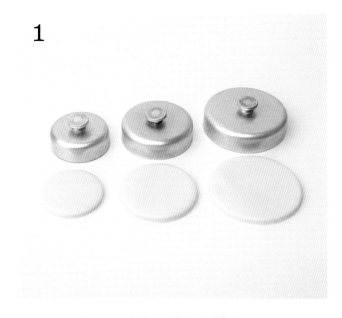

4

Tip I recommend using a silicone tool to smooth down the icing as a metal one can scratch the soft pastels and/or clay if you apply too much pressure.

9 To make the tree slice cake board, sandwich a thick layer of dark brown clay (or scrap clay) between two thin layers of light beige. Place the cake on top and use a craft knife to cut the shape, allowing a gap around the edge for decorations.

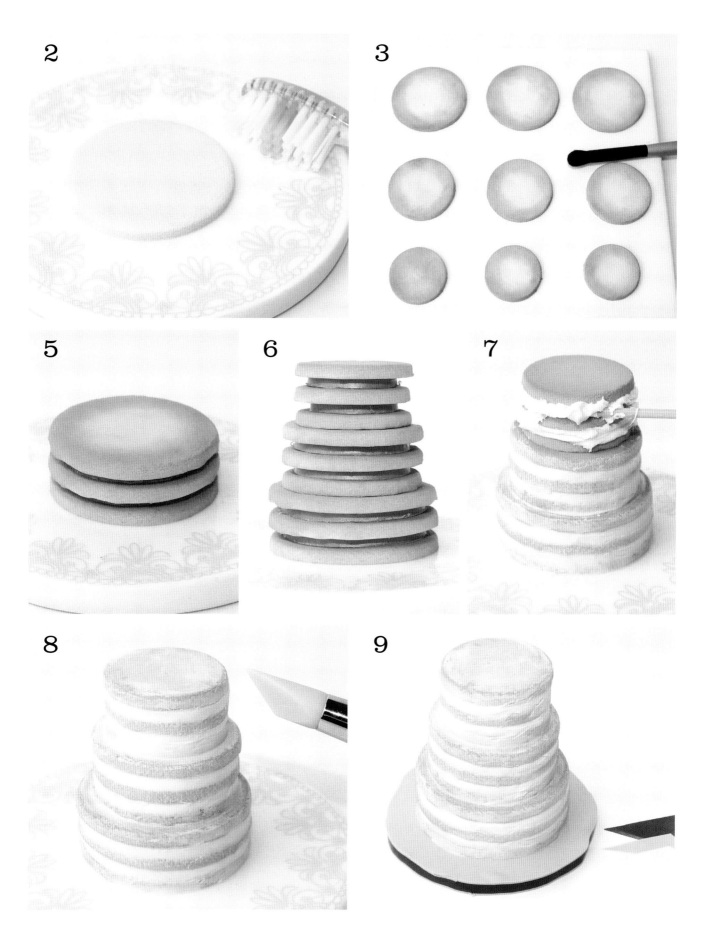

10 Remove the cake and roll a toothpick on the edges to create the tree bark texture. You can create dents and crevices in the clay by varying the pressure. Then use a toothbrush in a circular brushing motion to create the age lines in the tree.

11 Dust talcum powder on the clay and turn it over to texture the other side. The talcum powder cushions the texture as it goes inside the grooves, but still make sure to texture the clay gently to avoid damaging it. Part-bake.

12 Once cool, wash the talcum powder away and pat dry. Use your finger to rub some warm brown acrylic paint on the tree slice; the paint will go in all the lines you created with the toothbrush, resulting in natural highlights of ecru clay. You can repeat this as many times as you want, depending on how dark you want it to be. When the paint is dry, bond the cake to the tree slice with liquid polymer clay and part-bake.

13 Make some chocolate icing (see page 22) and spread it on all the tiers. Then use a dotting tool to pick up more icing to create the drips. You can either drag the clay down the side of the cake or, if the icing is stretchy enough for you to pick up a 'strand', place it on the cake and round up the end of the drip with the dotting tool. Part-bake.

14 Take a little pink, orange and purple polymer clay to tint three separate pieces of translucent clay. Roll them into thin strands and cut out lots of pieces to make the rose petals.

15 Roll the pieces into balls and flatten them, making one side as thin as you can.

16 Start by securing a small amount of clay on the end of a toothpick, then take a small petal and wrap it around the tip.

10

13

17 Overlap the following petal halfway across the previous one and keep it quite closed to make the centre of the rose appear tight.

18 Place the following petals slightly overlapping the previous ones. Add ones that gradually increase in size, especially when adding the last round.

11

12

14

15

16

17

18

19 To curl the edges of the petals, gently pinch them and/or curl the clay with your nails or a soft tool. To make the outer petals more open, press them at the base only and curl them.

20 To make a bud or a closed flower, keep the petals tighter around the core and don't curl them as much or at all.

21 Gently squeeze the base of the flower, pushing it upwards to release it from the toothpick and to secure the petals in place at the same time.

22 Use scissors or a blade to cut the excess clay and give the flower a flat base. Make as many flowers as you want, and choose the best-looking ones.

23 Take some green clay and shape it into a dome. You will have to measure this on the cake and allow space for the roses. Pick up the flowers by slightly pushing a toothpick into the centre and press them into the green clay, starting from the edge to achieve a neater finish. Turn the toothpick as you pull away to release the roses.

24 Place the rest of the roses and part-bake.

25 Once the centrepiece is baked and cool, place it on top of the cake, bonding with liquid polymer clay. Dab a little more liquid polymer clay where you want your other flowers to go, then arrange them. Part-bake.

26 Make some leaves (see page 88) and add them behind the roses, bonding with a little liquid polymer clay. If making little vines or leaves poking through the roses, dip them in liquid polymer clay first and nudge them in place. Bake one last time.

27 Once baked and cool, paint the tree bark a dark brown colour and dry-brush a little white acrylic paint with a flat brush so as not to get any paint in the grooves. Highlight the roses as well. As a last touch, dab a little glaze to stick on some nail caviar. Glaze the chocolate drips and tree slice.

19

22

25

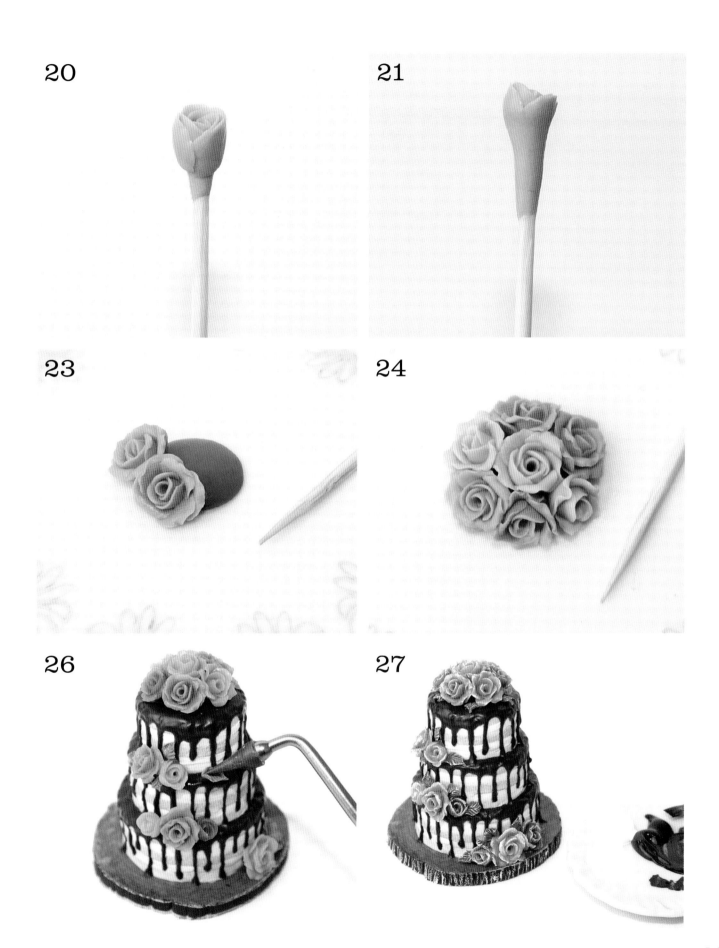

20

21

23

24

26

27

NAKED WEDDING CAKE 131

Topsy Turvy Cake

THIS IS ONE OF THE TRICKIEST CAKES TO MAKE BECAUSE OF THE SHAPE. HOWEVER, IF YOU GET THE FOUNDATIONS RIGHT, YOU CAN CREATE CAKES FOR ALL OCCASIONS, FROM A DELICATE CAKE WITH CHERRY BLOSSOM FLOWERS LIKE THE ONE SHOWN HERE, TO A WHIMSICAL CREATION PERFECT FOR A MAD HATTER'S TEA PARTY.

YOU WILL NEED

- Polymer clay in white (I used Sculpey Ultra Light), dark brown (I used Premo in Burnt Umber; otherwise use the colour of your choice to make the cake) and light pink

- Liquid polymer clay (I used FIMO Liquid)

- Acrylic paints in fuchsia and white

- Matte and gloss varnish

- Pasta machine or rolling pin

- Round cutters in three different sizes

- Pencil

- Blades

- Sandpaper

- Silicone mould putty

- Nail art drill

- Wire

- Pliers

- Small paintbrush

- Dotting tool

- Tapered silicone tool

1 Take some soft white polymer clay and put it through the thickest setting of your pasta machine. Stack three towers of around five layers each and push the cutters into the clay. I used Sculpey Ultra Light: this is less dense than regular polymer clay, so allows you to bake it in thicker layers without cracking, and is also easier to cut. Make the tiers a little higher than you'd want the cakes to be, as you'll be trimming some of it off.

2 Remove the excess clay from around the cutters and part-bake the cake tiers inside them (see page 13) to preserve the shape.

3 Once baked and cool, slide the cakes out a bit and use the cutter to hold the clay while you cut it. Use a pencil to draw a diagonal line across the top and a blade to carefully cut through the clay. Repeat with the other tiers. Wet-sand any imperfections if necessary.

4 Take some silicone mould putty and make moulds of the three tiers.

5 Fill in the moulds with dark brown clay to make a chocolate cake, or use another colour if you prefer. Part-bake the cakes in the moulds and let them cool. Wet-sand any rough edges and imperfections if necessary.

6 Use a nail art drill to make a hole in the centre of the bottom tier and the base of the middle tier. Do the same with the middle and top tier. The hole need not be deep; a few millimetres is enough.

7 Add a short piece of wire in the holes so that the cake layers don't move too much during baking.

8 Mix the same dark brown clay (or colour of your choice) with a little liquid polymer clay to obtain a cream consistency (see page 22). Spread a little around the wire so that the cakes stick together. Applying just liquid polymer clay may result in the liquid running down the cake while baking.

1

4

NOTE

Baking the polymer clay inside the moulds seems to protect it from direct heat, therefore allowing it to cure without splitting. If you still have splits or cracks, try building the cake out of Sculpey Ultra Light, covering the tiers in fondant or decorations where needed to hide imperfections.

5

6

7

8

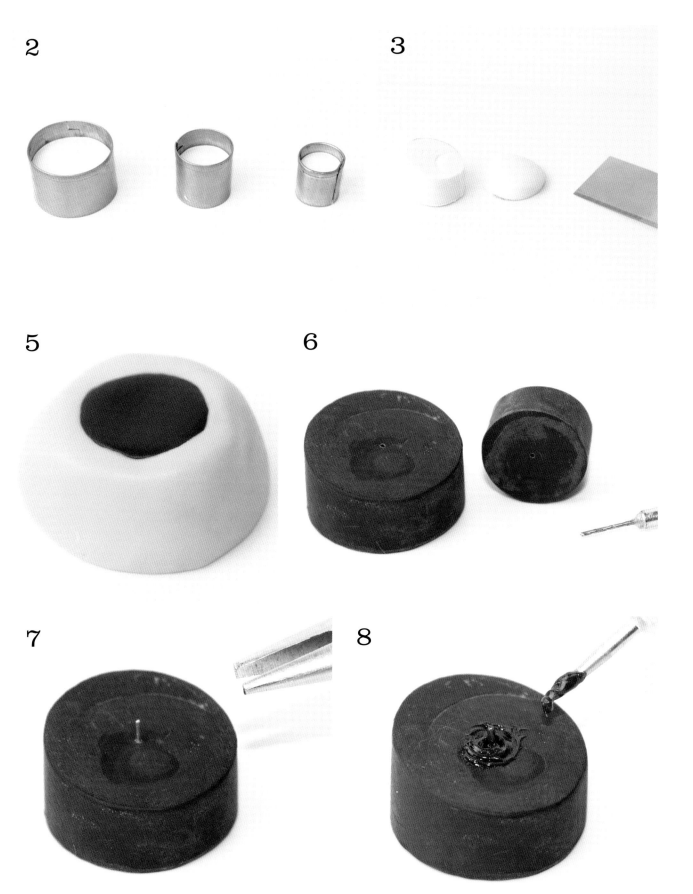

9 Connect all the tiers together and part-bake.

10 Make the flower petals while the cake is baking. Take some light pink clay and roll it into a thin strand. Cut lots of pieces and roll them into balls.

11 Flatten the balls into petal shapes and slide a blade underneath to lift off your work surface.

12 When the cake is out of the oven and cool, spread a little liquid polymer clay where you want the cherry blossoms to go. Pick up five petals and arrange them in a circle on the cake, slightly overlapping them.

Tip If you start overlapping the petals in a clockwise pattern, continue to do so; conversely, if you start in an anticlockwise pattern, continue in the same direction to make a harmonious-looking flower.

13 Add more cherry blossoms to the cake. Gradually make them smaller as you get near the top by decreasing the size of the petals. Bake.

14 Take some fuchsia acrylic paint and mix it with a little water. Pick up a very small amount of paint and dab it in the centre of the flowers, blending the colour outwards.

15 Water down some white acrylic paint and use a small dotting tool to dab dots around the flowers. Once all the paint is dry, glaze the flowers with matte varnish and the cake with gloss varnish.

9

12

15

Cinnamon Bun Ring

A CINNAMON BUN IS THE PERFECT PLACE TO START TURNING YOUR POLYMER CLAY FOOD INTO UNIQUE ITEMS OF JEWELLERY, AS IT REQUIRES SIMPLE MATERIALS WITHOUT COMPROMISING ON THE DELICIOUS RESULT. REMEMBER, YOU CAN MIX AND MATCH THE PROJECTS IN THIS BOOK AS YOU PLEASE, SO IF YOU DON'T FEEL LIKE MAKING JEWELLERY, YOU CAN TAKE ON THE CHALLENGE OF MAKING A MINI BAKING SCENE.

YOU WILL NEED

- Polymer clay in beige (I used FIMO Professional Doll Art), light brown (I used Premo in Raw Sienna), yellow and white

- Ring blank

- Soft pastels in browns

- Clear craft sand

- Liquid polymer clay (I used FIMO Liquid)

- Acrylic paints in warm brown tones

- Cinnamon fragrance (optional)

- Gloss varnish

- Tin foil

- Toothbrush

- Dotting tools

- Toothpick

- Needle tool

- Small paintbrush

1 Mix the beige polymer clay with a little light brown and yellow. Alternatively, you could use the Victoria sponge cake mix (see page 36) and add a little light brown.

2 Fill in the ring blank with this clay.

3 Place a ball of clay on the ring and around the edges. Use a ball of tin foil and a toothbrush to texture the bun.

4 Using a small dotting tool, trace a spiral starting from the centre. When you get near the edge, trace a line going down.

5 To create more detail, snap a toothpick in half and poke the jagged end into the clay to texture the edges of the groove.

6 To make the cinnamon bun look baked, dust soft pastels on it as described on page 19.

7 Use a needle tool to texture the inside of the groove by poking tiny holes and lines where the dough would naturally stretch while baking.

8 Mix clear craft sand, brown soft pastels and liquid polymer clay to create a brown sugar and cinnamon mix. You could add a couple of drops of cinnamon fragrance (see page 26) at this point. Spread the mix on the groove and part-bake the bun (see page 13).

Tip To bake the ring, scrunch some tin foil around the base to act as a support.

9 Let the ring cool down, then use acrylic paints in warm brown tones to further shade the bun. You could also apply brown paint in the groove to emphasize the cinnamon and sugar mix. Let the paint dry completely.

10 Make some white icing mix (see page 22) and spread it on the bun as neatly or as messily as you like. Bake one last time. Let cool, then glaze.

1

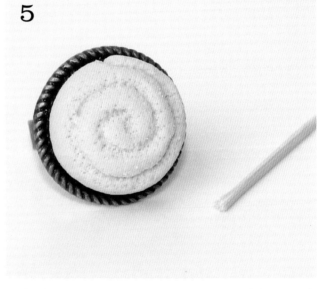

5

8

2

3

4

6

7

9

10

Doughnut Earrings

MAKING DOUGHNUTS IS FUN BECAUSE THERE ARE SO MANY WAYS TO DECORATE THEM. ONE OF MY FAVOURITE LOOKS IS THAT OF HOMEMADE, RUSTIC DOUGHNUTS, WITH LASHINGS OF ICING RUNNING DOWN THE SIDES AND BURSTING WITH COLOUR. IN THIS PROJECT WE WILL MAKE EARRINGS WITH TRIOS OF DOUGHNUTS, JUST TO PUSH OUR BOUNDARIES A LITTLE.

YOU WILL NEED

- Polymer clay in white, yellow, translucent and light brown (I used Premo in Raw Sienna) for the doughnuts; pink, dark brown and white for the icing (or any colours you like)

- Pasta machine or rolling pin

- Headpins

- Soft pastels in earth tones

- Liquid polymer clay (I used FIMO Liquid)

- Nail caviar

- Gloss varnish

- Earring wires

- Blades/knife

- Small paintbrush

- Dotting tool

- Detail tool

- Toothbrush

- Jewellery pliers: flat-nose, round-nose and side cutters

1   Mix white polymer clay with a little yellow and raw sienna to obtain a warm light yellow. Then mix in some translucent clay, roll out a thin strand and cut six even pieces to make the doughnuts.

2   Roll the pieces into balls and flatten them a little.

3   Using the end of a brush handle, gently poke a hole through the clay till you get to the other side, then turn the piece over and repeat to make a neat hole. Spin the brush to release it from the clay if it gets stuck.

4   Using a detail tool, trace a line around the middle of the doughnut – it doesn't have to be straight or neat. Use the detail tool to texture that line by poking little holes, creating tears and crevices in the dough.

5   Carefully push a headpin through the inside of two of the doughnuts (these will be the top ones), keeping the headpin at an angle to avoid scraping the clay.

Tip I like to feel for the headpin breaking through the clay with my index finger, as this helps preserve the shape a little.

6   Carefully pull the headpin through to the other side and push the head into the clay a little.

7   Use a toothbrush to add texture to the doughnuts.

8   To make the doughnuts look golden, apply a dusting of soft pastels in a light terracotta colour. I mixed a little of the darkest beige in my set of pastels with the terracotta and dusted that on the doughnuts, trying to avoid the line running around the centre.

9   Arrange the doughnuts in any position you like and apply a little liquid polymer clay between them. Do this on your baking tray to avoid having to transfer them onto another one and distorting your work. Part-bake (see page 13).

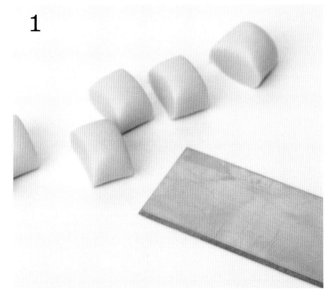

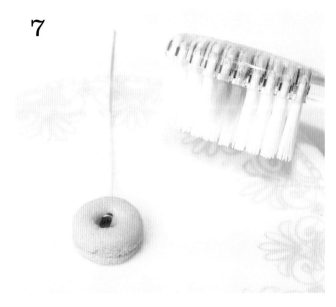

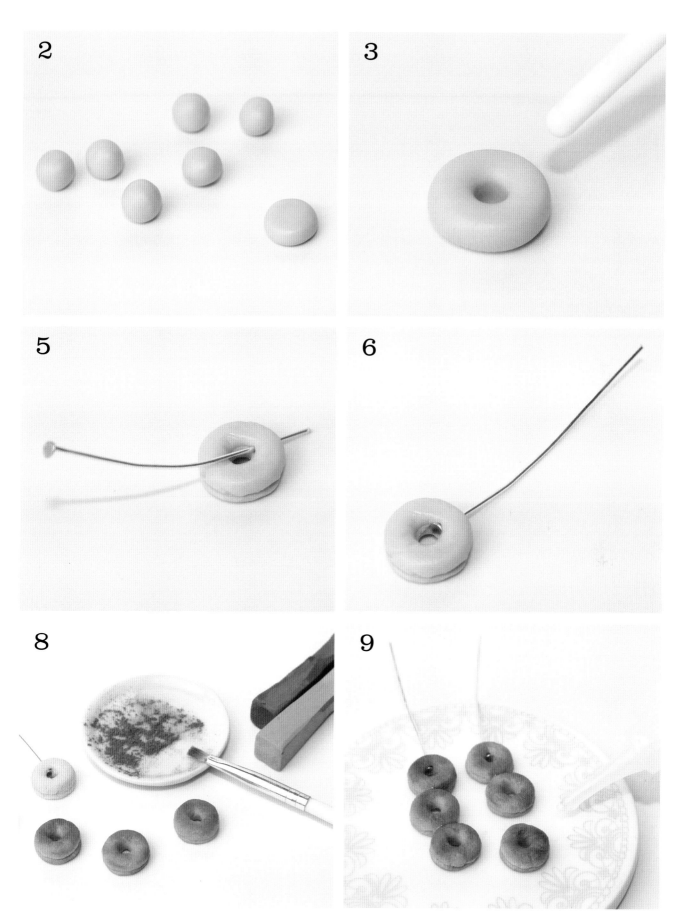

10 Once your doughnuts are out of the oven and cool, make some pink and white icing (see page 22) and apply it to the top and bottom doughnuts respectively.

11 Take some nail caviar in your favourite colours and mix together. Sprinkle over the doughnuts so the look is as random as on real doughnuts. Do this over a bowl or deep tray because the nail caviar like to bounce around. Bake again for another 10–15 minutes.

12 Make some chocolate icing and apply it to the middle doughnuts. Then, using a small dotting tool, pick up some white icing; when it stretches into a very thin strand, lay it across the chocolate icing. Don't drag it; just carefully lay it down. Bake again for 30 minutes.

13 Apply a coat of glaze to the doughnuts and let it dry completely. Once dry, take some flat nose pliers and hold the wire at the base, then use your finger to push the wire over the pliers into a 90-degree angle.

14 Hold the wire by the fold with the round-nose pliers in a perpendicular position and push the wire over the pliers until it points to the other side.

15 Turn the pliers sideways and continue pulling the wire down, then past the doughnuts to create an eye.

16 Hold the eye with flat-nose pliers and wrap the wire around and behind the neck.

17 Wrap the wire a couple of times around the neck or as many times as you can in the space.

18 Trim the excess wire with side cutters. If any wire is sticking out, tuck it in with flat-nose pliers.

19 Link the charms to earring wires. You can apply a second coat of gloss varnish to the icing to make the doughnuts look extra-shiny and delicious.

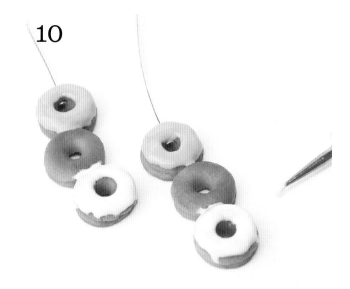

10

13

17

11

12

14

15

16

18

19

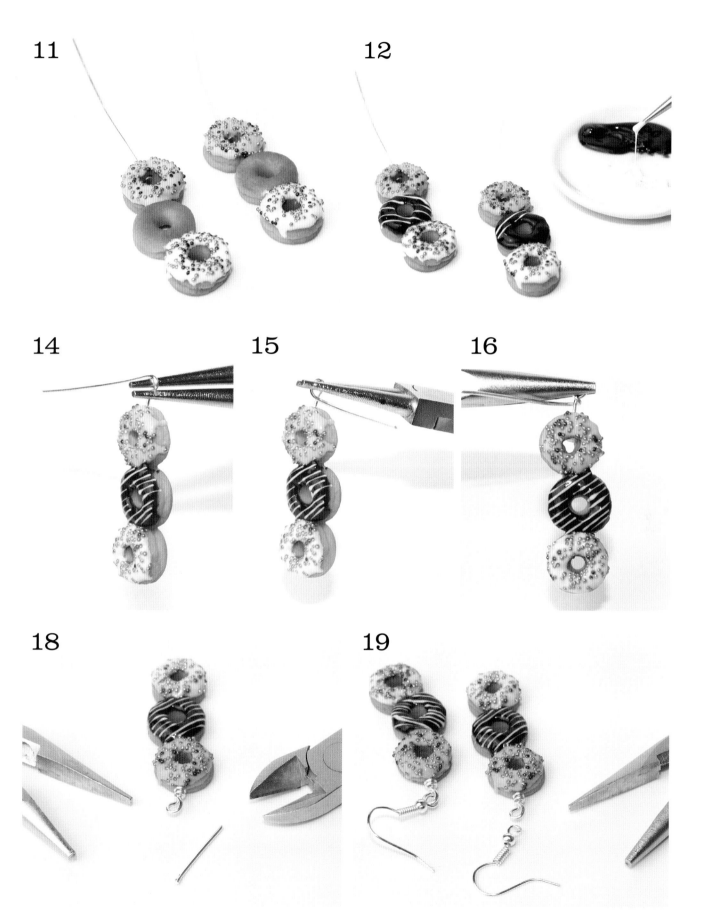

Triple Chocolate Cookie Stud Earrings

IN THIS PROJECT I WILL SHOW YOU HOW YOU CAN TURN YOUR POLYMER CLAY FOOD PIECES INTO STUD EARRINGS. THE CHOCOLATE CHIP COOKIES ARE MERELY A DELICIOUS EXCUSE TO MAKE SOME JEWELLERY.

YOU WILL NEED

- Polymer clay in light brown (I used Premo in Raw Sienna), dark brown (I used Premo in Burnt Umber), light yellow, translucent and Victoria sponge cake mix (see page 36)

- Soft pastels in beige

- Acrylic paints in beige and browns

- Cyanoacrylate glue

- Earring posts

- Gloss varnish

- Blade

- Craft knife

- Tin foil

- Toothbrush

- Dotting tool

- Soft brush

- Small paintbrush

1 Part-bake thin strands of polymer clay in the following colours to make the chocolate chips: light brown to make the milk chocolate, dark brown to make the dark chocolate, and light yellow mixed with roughly the same amount of translucent to make the white chocolate. Once baked and cool, chop the pieces up.

2 Take some polymer clay in the Victoria sponge cake mix and mix in the chocolate chips. If you add more translucent clay, the cookies will look more buttery. Don't add too much or they can end up looking greasy.

3 Roll the clay into a cylinder and cut as many equal-sized pieces as you want cookies.

4 Roll the pieces into balls and flatten them. Scrunch a small amount of tin foil into a ball and roll it on the cookies to create some texture.

5 Now take a toothbrush and stipple it all over the cookies. To create deeper grooves, wiggle the tip of the brush where the cookies naturally dip.

6 Take the lightest beige colour in your soft pastel set and apply a very light dusting with a soft brush. Bake.

7 Once the cookies are out of the oven and cool, take acrylic paints in beige and warm browns and mix them with a little water. Apply the lightest colour around the edge of the cookies, blending it towards the centre. Dip the tip of the brush in the warm brown and apply it around the bottom edge, blending it upwards. When the paint is dry, you can go back over it with a small amount of dry brown if you want.

8 If you want your cookies dipped in chocolate, make some dark brown icing (see page 22), spread a little on one half of them and bake.

9 Take a craft knife and scratch the surface of the earring posts and the base of the cookies. This will create a rough surface that will make the glue adhere better.

1

4

7

10 Dab a small dot of glue on the back of the cookie and place the earring post. You can help hold the post in position with a dotting tool.

11 Apply a small amount of gloss varnish on the cookies to give them a little shine.

2

3

5

6

8

9

10

11

TRIPLE CHOCOLATE COOKIE STUD EARRINGS   151

Meringue Kiss Pins

USING VERY FEW MATERIALS, HERE I'LL GUIDE YOU THROUGH THE MAKING OF MERINGUE KISSES AND HOW TO TURN THEM INTO PINS TO ATTACH TO YOUR CLOTHES OR BAGS. IF RAINBOWS ARE NOT TO YOUR TASTE, USE YOUR FAVOURITE COLOUR COMBINATION INSTEAD.

YOU WILL NEED

- Polymer clay in white

- Soft pastels in the colours of the rainbow

- Liquid polymer clay (I used FIMO Liquid)

- Pin blanks

- Acrylic paint in white

- Gloss varnish (optional)

- Tapered silicone sculpting tool

- Small round brush

- Nail art drill or craft knife (if required)

- Small flat brush

1 Roll some white polymer clay into a ball roughly the size of a big marble.

2 Turn the ball and pinch the top to make the pointy shape typical of meringue kisses. Gently push the clay down as you pinch it to make it flatter.

3 Curl the tip of the meringue and use a tapered silicone tool to create grooves to make it look piped. I take advantage of the shape of the tool and push it down vertically on the clay (narrow end up) and gently roll it from side to side to open the groove and to soften the edges.

4 Once you have sculpted the whole meringue kiss, run the silicone tool up the grooves to add a little more definition and tidy up the base. You don't need to trace the lines all the way up to the tip of the meringue; let them fade away.

5 To make the meringue kiss burst with colour, take some soft pastels in the colours of the rainbow and scrape some onto a piece of paper or dish. Use a round brush to pick up the colour and gently stipple it on the meringue. Don't be afraid to overlap the colours, as that will create a gradient effect. Part-bake (see page 13).

Tip Soft pastels appear much lighter on polymer clay after baking, so applying a second coat will help them look brighter.

6 Spread liquid polymer clay on the base of the meringue and a little on the pin blank. Place the pin blank on the base and press a strip of white clay on it, blending the clay towards the edges. Bake.

7 If you want to cover the whole base of the pin with clay, you'll need to make space for the 'tail' for it to close properly. You can close it and open it again before baking it so that the tail goes into the clay, creating the space for it. If the clay gets in the way of the pin closing, you can make space for it using a nail art drill or a knife after baking.

1

8 To highlight the highest points of the meringue, take some white acrylic paint and use a flat brush in a horizontal position. Wipe the excess paint away first to avoid adding too much to the meringue. If you do add too much, let it dry for a couple of minutes, then use a clean brush to tidy up the edges and blur them away.

ALTERNATIVE COLOURING METHOD

You don't have to apply soft pastels all over; you could just apply them to the highest points, as I did here. I applied a little loose soft pastel first; then, once the piece was baked, I applied soft pastel pencils in matching colours while the clay was still warm and rubbed them in with my fingers. Apply a thin coat or two of glaze (letting the glaze dry in between applications) for extra shine. You could also sprinkle white glitter dust on the meringues before the glaze dries.

Confetti Cupcake Earrings

I LOVE FOOD THAT'S BURSTING WITH COLOUR, AND IN THIS PROJECT I'LL SHOW YOU HOW TO MAKE FUN VANILLA CUPCAKE EARRINGS WITH LOTS AND LOTS OF SPRINKLES. I FEEL THAT YOU SHOULD HAVE A PAIR OF THESE EITHER IN YOUR JEWELLERY OR MINI CUPCAKE COLLECTION.

YOU WILL NEED

- Polymer clay in yellow, white and translucent, and different colours to make the sprinkles

- Silicone mould putty

- Soft pastel in beige

- Acrylic paint in beige, raw sienna, brown and white

- Nail caviar

- Cyanoacrylate glue

- Screw eye bails

- Earring wires

- Gloss varnish

- Toothbrush

- Soft brush

- Small paintbrush

- Craft knife/blades

- Flat-ended tool

- Dotting tool

- Nail art drill

- Flat-nose pliers

1 Mix yellow and white clay to obtain a pastel tint and mix a speck of it with some translucent clay. Make a cupcake mould as in the project on page 56. Once ready, take your cupcake mould and fill it to the top with the clay mix.

2 Take the pastel yellow mix and add some more translucent clay. Roll it into a ball and press it onto the cupcake.

Tip I like to use translucent clay in cakes and cupcakes to create the illusion of sugar and butter. You can use the Victoria sponge cake mix too (see page 36). If your mix looks too cold and yellow, try adding a little raw sienna.

3 Use a toothbrush to texture the cupcake top.

4 Scrape a little beige soft pastel and gently brush it on the cupcake. Make a second cupcake and part-bake (see page 13).

5 Once cool, remove the cupcakes from the moulds and apply a little beige acrylic paint on two-thirds of the cupcake liner.

6 Mix raw sienna and brown acrylic paints together and mix a little of that with the beige colour. Apply a small amount to the bottom edge of the cupcake liner and blend it upwards. I like to go back in with this colour and stipple it so that it creates an uneven look. You can also paint the cupcakes as described in the project on page 58.

7 Mix a little beige and raw sienna together and mix with water to create a wash. Pick up a tiny amount and brush it along the edge of the cupcake top. If you apply too much, blend the excess with a clean damp brush.

1

4

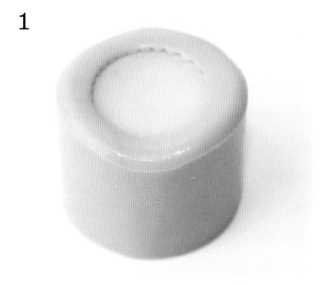

8 Once the paint is dry, load a brush with some white acrylic paint. Brush the excess paint away to make the bristles flat, still leaving enough paint on the brush. Keep the brush in a horizontal position and stipple it on the highest points of the cupcake liner.

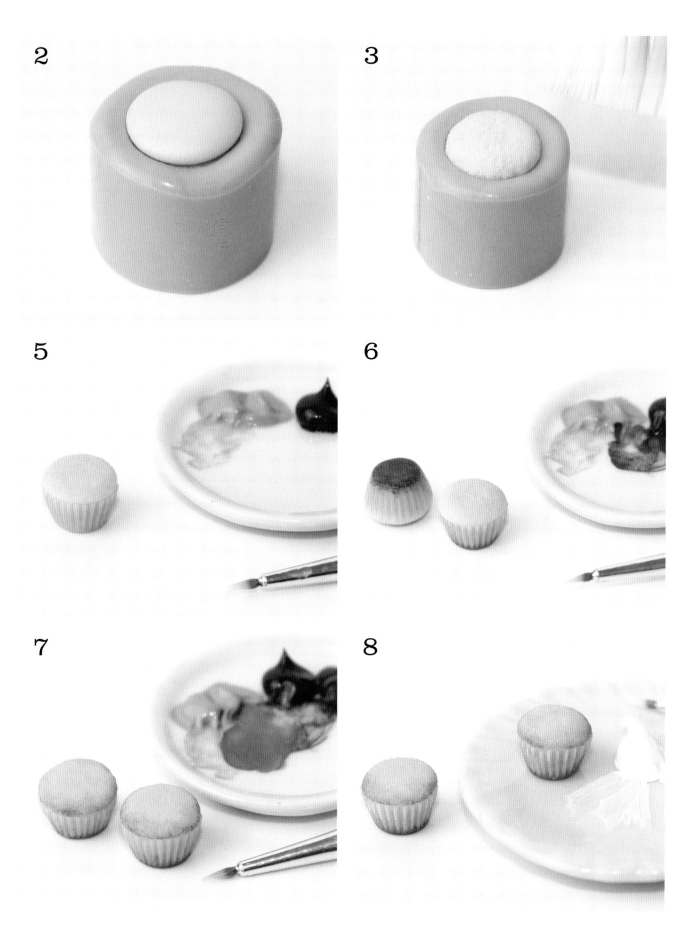

2

3

5

6

7

8

9 Take polymer clay in a selection of colours and roll it into very thin strands. Part-bake the strands and chop them up to make the sprinkles.

10 Make some buttercream (see page 22) and spread it on the cupcakes. I used a mix of white and yellow, but you can use any colour you like.

Tip Use a flat-ended tool to apply the buttercream to make it look as if it has been spread with a spatula.

11 Add your sprinkles and any other decorations you want such as nail caviar. Use a dotting tool to gently push them into the icing, then bake.

12 Once your cupcakes are out of the oven and cool, drill a hole into the centre using a nail art drill.

13 Brush a little strong glue on the screw eye bail before screwing it in place.

14 Link your cupcakes to your earring wires using flat-nose pliers, then apply gloss varnish. You can hang the cupcakes from a brush handle over a bowl to let them dry.

9

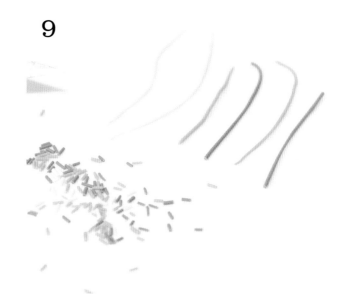

12

10

11

13

14

CONFETTI CUPCAKE EARRINGS

Brownies and Ice-Cream Charms

BROWNIES AND ICE CREAM ARE A STAPLE WHEN IT COMES TO DESSERTS.
IT DOESN'T MATTER IF YOU'VE NEVER TRIED MAKING SUCH A PROJECT BEFORE;
THESE EASY STEPS WILL HELP YOU ACHIEVE YOUR FIRST POLYMER CLAY
BROWNIES AND ICE CREAM WITH MOUTH-WATERING RESULTS.

YOU WILL NEED

- Polymer clay in dark brown (I used Premo in Burnt Umber) and light brown (I used Premo in Raw Sienna) for the brownie; pastel pink and a little pre-baked red for the ice cream

- Headpin

- Liquid polymer clay (I used FIMO Liquid)

- Nail caviar

- Bead

- Gloss varnish

- Strawberry fragrance

- Pasta machine or rolling pin

- Ruler

- Blade

- Toothbrush

- Needle tool/fine-ended tool

- Craft knife

- Dotting tool

- Mini grater

- Flat tool or toothpick

- Jewellery pliers: flat-nose, round-nose and side cutters

1 To make the brownies, stack two sheets of clay together: dark brown (settings #1 and #4 stacked together) and light brown (setting #9 or thinnest). Cut a rectangle and use a ruler to mark ⅜in (1cm) squares.

2 Use a blade to cut the brownies.

3 Texture the top and sides of the brownies with a toothbrush. You can wiggle the tip of the brush into the clay to create dips and texture the clay at the same time.

4 Use a needle or fine-ended tool to create cracks on the top layer and to fluff up the edges. Pay special attention to the edges and corners, as these will be the most visible.

5 Carefully remove and/or lift small pieces of the top layer with a knife and texture the inside with a needle tool to make it look crumbly.

6 Make another two brownies, stack all three together and gently push a headpin through the centre of the stack. Part-bake for 15 minutes (see page 13).

7 Once baked and cool, remove the headpin, turn it over so that the head is at the bottom and then push it through the brownies again. This way the brownies run no risk of flying out of your findings. Spread a little liquid polymer clay on the top brownie.

8 To make the strawberry ice cream, mix pastel pink clay with grated pre-baked red clay.

1

4

6

9 Make a ball out of the strawberry clay and push it through the headpin.

10 Use a flat tool or a toothpick to flatten the edge of the ice-cream and secure it to the clay underneath.

11 After using a toothbrush to add general texture to the ice cream scoop, use a craft knife to score parallel lines. You can go back in with a toothbrush to soften them if necessary.

12 To make your ice cream look as if it is melting into the hot brownie, mix a little liquid polymer clay with some of the strawberry clay until it is runny. This would be a good time to add a few drops of strawberry fragrance if you like. Use a dotting tool to spread the mixture around the edges of the ice cream scoop and to drag it down to create the drips. Then blend it upwards with a brush.

13 Take some nail caviar in different colours to decorate the ice cream with sprinkles, and push them into the clay to secure them in place. Bake and let cool.

14 Trim the excess wire off the headpin with side cutters and add a bead – use a red one if you want it to look like a cherry.

15 Using round-nose pliers, bend the wire to create a hook shape. Keep coiling the wire until you reach the bead. Close the loose end with flat-nose pliers if necessary. Finish with a thin coat of gloss varnish and let it dry completely.

Strawberries and Cream Cake Earrings

STRAWBERRIES AND CREAM, WHETHER ON THEIR OWN OR IN A CAKE, ARE ONE OF MY FAVOURITE DESSERTS, AND I NEVER TIRE OF MAKING THEM OUT OF POLYMER CLAY. IN THIS PROJECT I'LL SHOW YOU HOW TO USE SCREW BAILS WITH POLYMER CLAY PIECES TO MAKE SIMPLE BUT CUTE CAKE EARRINGS THAT ARE PERFECT FOR THE SUMMER.

YOU WILL NEED

- Polymer clay in semi-translucent pink, darker pink, Victoria sponge cake mix (see page 36), white, translucent light yellow and leaf green

- Acrylic paints in red shades

- Screw eye bails

- Cyanoacrylate glue

- Jewellery wire

- Beads

- Earring wires

- Gloss varnish

- Pasta machine or rolling pin

- Round cutter

- Blades

- Needle tool

- Dotting tool

- Small flat brush

- Tweezers

- Nail art drill

- Jewellery pliers: flat-nose, round-nose and side cutters

1 Roll out a thick sheet of semi-translucent pink clay (setting #1), cut out two circles and 'brown' them with a darker shade of pink. You will also need one circle of Victoria sponge cake mix (browned; see page 18) and two circles of white clay.

2 Stack the layers together, with the white circles in between.

3 Cut the cake into eight slices to make four pairs of earrings.

4 Use a needle tool to texture the inside of the sponge and to tease the icing a little. Part-bake (see page 13).

5 Make the strawberries from translucent light yellow clay by rolling out a thin strand and cutting eight tiny pieces. Roll them into balls, then teardrops, and flatten them slightly, especially at the narrow end. Use a needle tool to poke tiny holes to create the effect of seeds.

6 Break up pieces of leaf green clay to make little strips. Use a dotting tool to add them to the strawberries in perpendicular positions to create the leaves. Part-bake and leave to cool.

7 Paint the strawberries with red acrylic paint, using a flat brush to emphasize the seeds. Use a darker red to shade the tip of the strawberry, blending the paint upwards. Let dry completely.

Tip Wipe away excess paint when picking it up to avoid getting blobs of paint in the seeds.

8 Make some white cream (see page 22) and use it to cover the baked and cooled cake slices. Place one strawberry in the middle of each slice, gently pressing it into the cream. If you want to attach the earring wires at the top, place the strawberries slightly forward. Bake for 30 minutes.

1

4

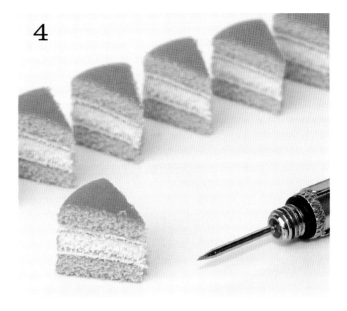

7

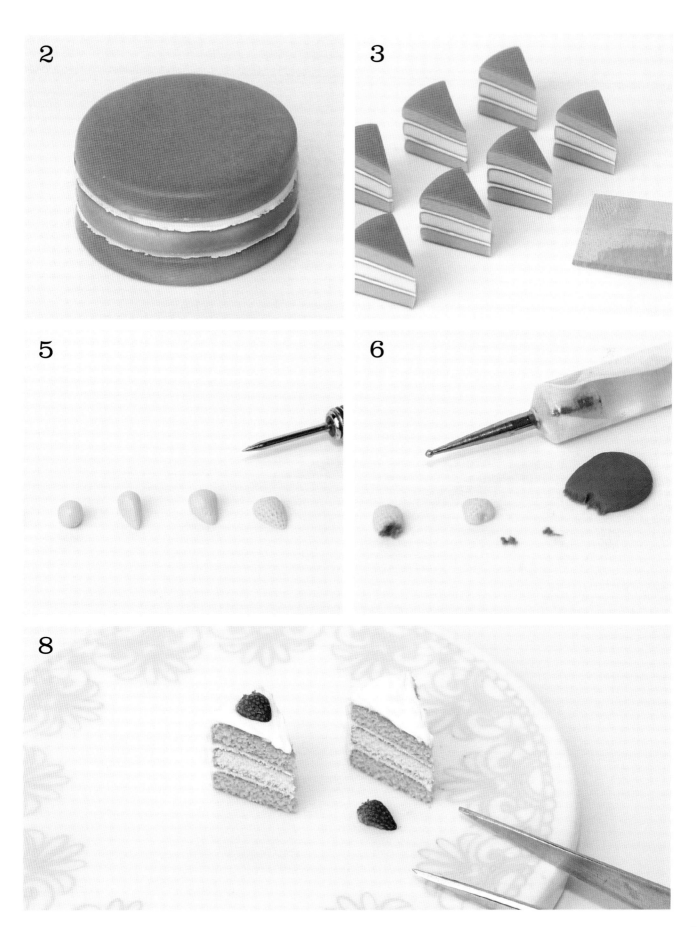

9 Drill holes on the back of the slices using a small nail art hand drill. Make sure the hole is not too big for the jewellery findings.

10 Take some screw eye bails and screw them into the holes in a vertical position. For added strength, you can brush a little cyanoacrylate glue on them before securing them in place. If you end up with a lip of glue around the neck of the bail, wipe it off with a tissue or a toothpick.

11 Take a piece of jewellery wire. Using round-nose pliers, bend the end of the wire to create a loop.

12 Add a bead and trim off the excess wire with side cutters.

13 Hold the wire by the loop with flat-nose pliers and use the round-nose pliers to close the other end.

14 Open one end of the wire and link it to the cake slice (open the loop upwards instead of sideways to avoid distorting the round shape). Close it back up with flat-nose pliers, making sure there are no gaps for the findings to escape through.

15 Open the earring wire in the same way and attach it to the rest of the earring.

16 Glaze the strawberries with gloss varnish, and the cream if you like. Let them dry completely.

9

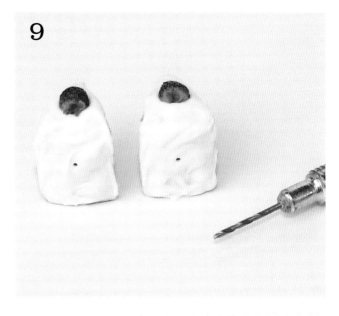

12

15

10

11

13

14

16

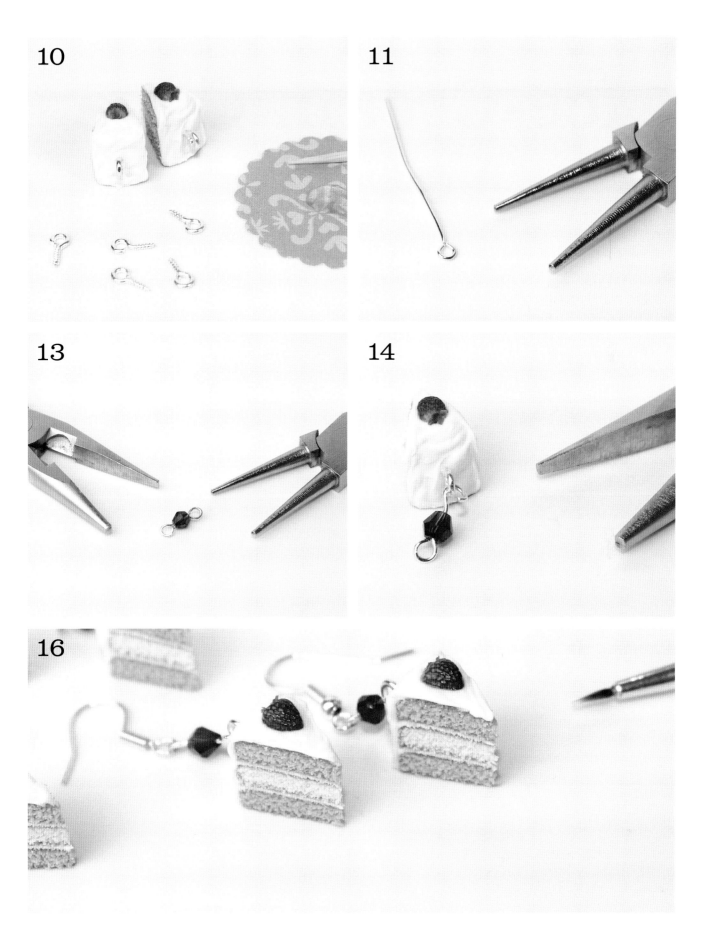

STRAWBERRIES AND CREAM CAKE EARRINGS 173

Ice-Cream Cone Necklace

NOTHING SAYS SUMMERTIME LIKE AN ICE-CREAM CONE WITH WONKY SCOOPS MELTING INTO EACH OTHER. TEXTURING POLYMER CLAY TO CREATE THE EFFECT OF ICE CREAM IS NOT ONLY FUN BUT ALSO A GREAT WAY TO SHAKE OFF FEARS ABOUT MAKING MISTAKES: EACH SCOOP OF ICE CREAM HAS ITS OWN IRREGULARITIES, MAKING EACH ONE PERFECT IN ITS OWN WAY.

YOU WILL NEED

- Polymer clay in light beige (I used Premo in Ecru) for the cone; mint (I used FIMO Effect), dark brown (pre-baked), pastel pink and pastel yellow for the ice cream; light green for the strawberry leaves

- Cornflour or talcum powder (if needed)

- Soft pastels in browns

- Liquid polymer clay (I used FIMO Liquid)

- Headpin

- Acrylic paints in pinks and brown

- Gloss and matte varnish

- Jewellery wire

- Beads that match the ice cream colours

- Necklace chain

- Jump rings

- Pasta machine or rolling pin

- Tool with cross-hatch grip

- Round cutter

- Toothbrush

- Tapered silicone tool or icing nozzle

- Toothpick

- Needle tool

- Tin foil

- Flat tool

- Dotting tool

- Jewellery pliers: flat-nose, round-nose and side cutters

- Paintbrush

1 Roll out a sheet of light beige polymer clay through the #5/6 setting of your pasta machine. Roll a tool with a cross-hatch grip on it to create the waffle pattern on the clay. If the clay sticks to your tool, dust a little cornflour or talcum powder on them and try again.

2 Cut out a circle. This can be any size you want, depending on how big you want your ice-cream cone to be.

3 Add a little texture with a toothbrush.

4 To make the cone look cooked and crispy, dust soft pastels in brown shades slightly unevenly. Make the cone look as light or dark as you want.

5 Roll the cone into itself; you can do this between your fingers or use a tapered silicone tool or icing nozzle. If you find the soft pastels prevent the clay from sticking, add a little liquid polymer clay.

6 Place the cone on an icing nozzle and use a toothpick or a needle tool to create some texture on the joint. Part-bake the cone (see page 13).

Tip You can use the icing nozzle as a base to bake the cone on or bake it on a sheet of standard A4 paper.

7 To make the mint chocolate chip ice cream, chop up a pre-baked thin strand of dark brown clay and mix it in with the mint polymer clay.

8 Roll the mint ice cream and your two other flavours into balls. I used pastel pink for strawberry and pastel yellow for vanilla, but feel free to make your favourite flavours.

9 Take your baked ice-cream cone, spread a little liquid polymer clay inside it, and fill it with your first ice-cream flavour. Push a headpin into the clay and tighten the clay around it.

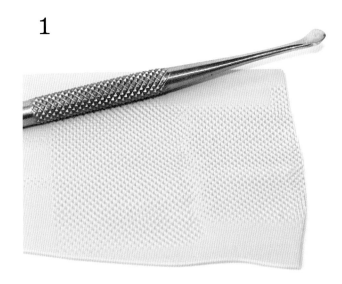

2

3

5

6

8

9

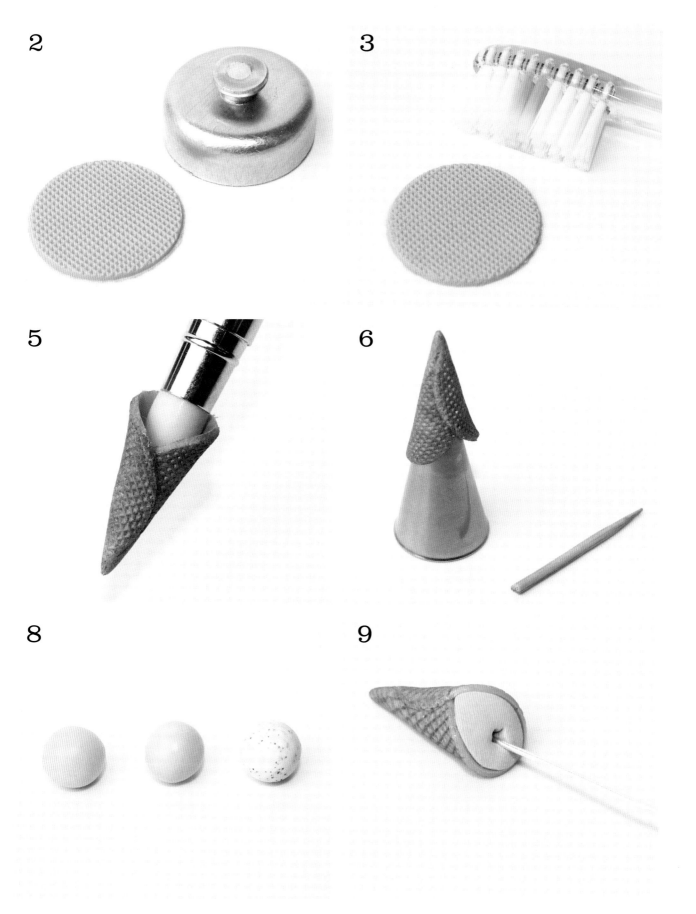

Tip Headpins are no longer than 2in (5cm) so should you wish to create an ice-cream cone with more than three scoops, use a piece of wire instead. Coil the end of the wire before inserting it into the clay (in step 9) so that it doesn't slide out of the clay once it's cured. Then assemble the ice-cream cone as described below.

10 Slide the first scoop of ice cream through the headpin and push it into the clay underneath. Scrunch up some tin foil around an icing nozzle to make a baking stand for the ice cream.

11 Use a toothpick to add general texture and to shape the scoop at the same time. Then lightly go over with a toothbrush and finally a needle tool, to fluff up the edges a little and to add details such as fine lines and tiny holes. Now part-bake the ice cream cone for 10 minutes.

12 Slide the second scoop of ice cream in place, offsetting it slightly, bonding it to the first one with a little liquid polymer clay. I used a flat tool to shape the top at an angle so that the last two scoops didn't look perfectly straight. Add texture to the ice cream and part-bake.

13 Add the third scoop slightly to the right so that it looks as if it is sliding off the vanilla, then add general texture with a toothpick and toothbrush.

14 Use the toothpick to shape the scoop further and a needle tool to texture the edges.

15 Mix liquid polymer clay with polymer clay in the same colour as the ice cream scoops until you have a consistency a little thinner than cream, but not as thin as icing (see page 22). Use a dotting tool to create the melting ice cream; drag the tool down to make the drips look as if they are melting into each other.

10

13

16 To make a strawberry, take a small piece of the same pastel yellow polymer clay used to make the vanilla ice cream and roll it into a teardrop. Flatten it slightly and use a needle tool to poke in holes to create the effect of the seeds.

17 Add pieces of light green clay to make the leaves, then bake for 10 minutes.

18 Once cool, apply a coat of light pink acrylic paint all over and a medium shade to the narrower half of the strawberry. Finish with a dark pink on the tip, blending it upwards.

19 Once the paint is dry, carefully push the strawberry into the top scoop, bonding with a little of the melted ice-cream mix. Bake.

20 To make the waffle cone appear even crispier, apply a small amount of warm brown acrylic paint on the highest points. Glaze the strawberry with gloss varnish and the cone with matte varnish. Let it dry completely.

21 Trim the excess wire with side cutters and close the loop with round-nose pliers.

22 Take a piece of jewellery wire and use round-nose pliers to create an eye. Slide on three beads in colours that match the ice cream.

23 Trim the excess wire and close the loop using round-nose pliers.

24 Make a second beaded wire and attach it to the ice-cream cone.

25 Take the necklace chain and remove one link from the centre. Take two jump rings and attach them to the ends of the chain using flat-nose pliers.

Tip You can hammer the jump rings a little if you like a rustic and uneven look.

26 Connect the jump rings to the ice cream cone. The necklace is ready.

18

21

24

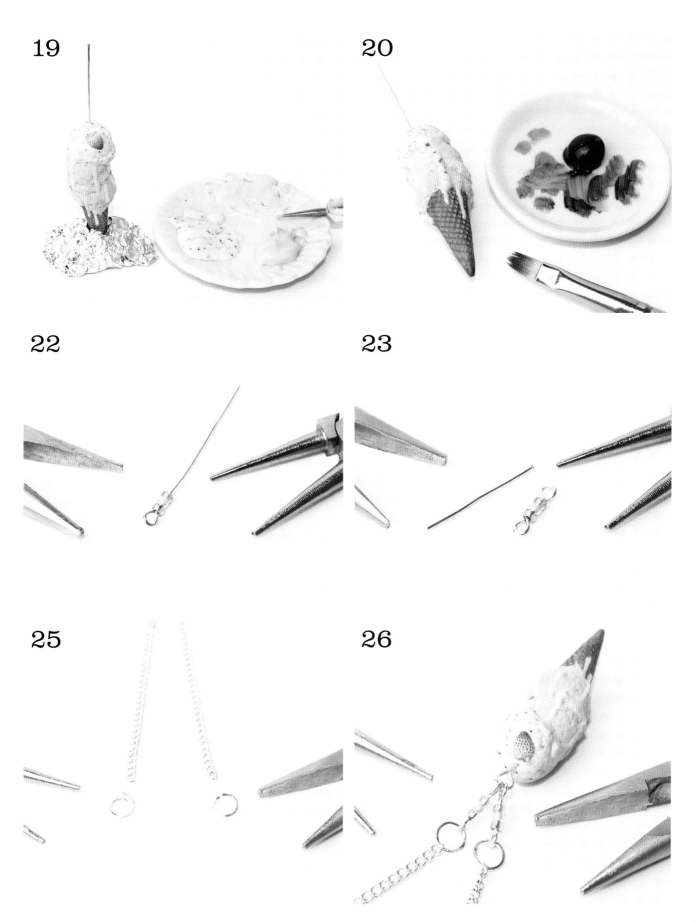

Bitten Cupcake Bag Charm

I LOVE A CUPCAKE THAT LOOKS IRRESISTIBLE, SO WHAT BETTER WAY OF CONVEYING THAT THAN WITH A CUPCAKE WITH A MOUTHFUL MISSING, OOZING WITH BUTTERCREAM AND JAM? LET'S GET STARTED ON ONE OF THE MOST DELICIOUS ACCESSORIES YOU'LL EVER MAKE.

YOU WILL NEED

- Polymer clay in dark brown (I used Premo in Burnt Umber), light yellow, light pink, leaf green, red and translucent

- Acrylic paint in red

- Liquid polymer clay (I used FIMO Liquid)

- Craft sand

- Gloss varnish

- Eye screw bails

- Cyanoacrylate glue

- Keyring

- Spoon charm (optional)

- Jump ring

- Silicone mould putty

- Toothbrush

- Blade

- Dotting tool

- Pointy metal tool

- Needle tool

- Toothpick

- Small paintbrush

- Tapered silicone tool

- Detail tool

- Nail art hand drill

- Round- and flat-nose pliers

1 Make a cupcake mould (see page 27) and fill it with dark brown polymer clay to make a chocolate cupcake.

2 Add a ball of dark brown clay on top and flatten it into a dome, making sure none of the base is exposed, and texture it with a toothbrush.

3 Let the clay rest in the mould for a little while if it's too soft, then carefully remove it from the mould. Use a blade to remove a chunk.

Tip Sometimes I use a straw or a small daisy-shaped cutter to remove individual sections from the cupcake so that they look like teeth marks. This works best when the clay is firm, as you could squash it in the process.

4 Use a dotting tool to poke a hole in the centre of the cupcake to create space for the jam later on.

5 Texture the inside of the cupcake with a needle tool to make it look like cake crumbs.

6 Texture the outside of the cupcake liner by gently scratching and fluffing up the surface. Part-bake (see page 13).

7 To make the strawberry, take a ball of light yellow clay and shape it into a teardrop. Round off the edges and place the strawberry on the end of a toothpick. Using a pointy metal tool, poke lots of holes to create the effect of the seeds. Part-bake.

8 Once the strawberry is baked and cool, dry brush red acrylic paint on it until it is completely covered.

9 Let the paint dry completely. Make some chocolate icing (see page 22) and apply it on about half the strawberry. Part-bake.

1

4

7

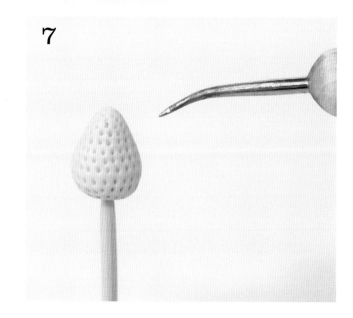

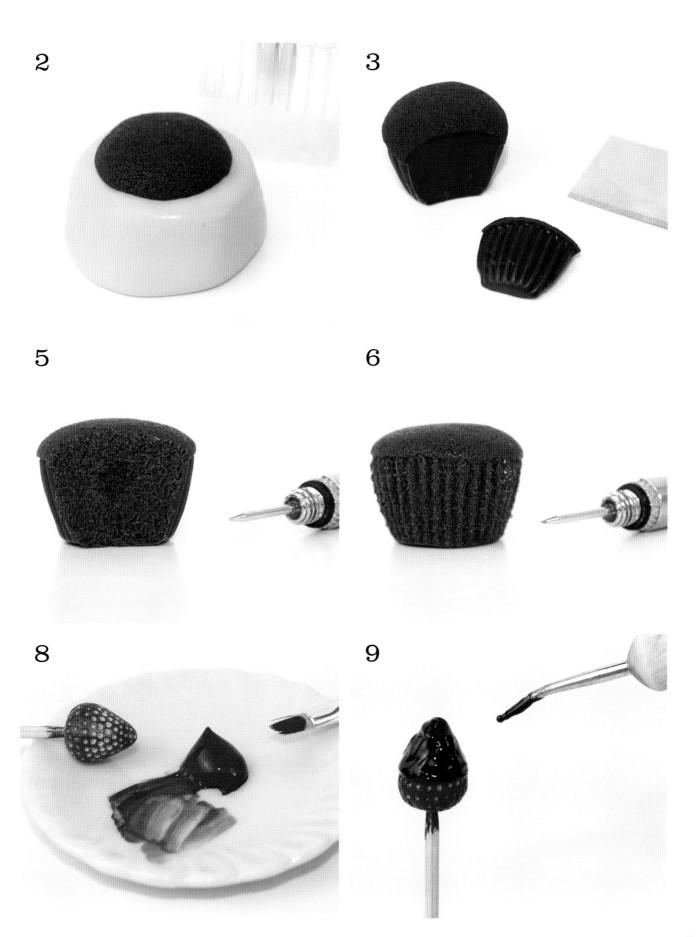

10 Make some light pink buttercream (see page 22) and spread it on the cupcake, dragging some of it downwards.

11 Place the strawberry on the buttercream. Part-bake.

12 To make the strawberry leaves, roll small balls of leaf green clay into teardrops and place them on top of the strawberry, bonding with a little liquid polymer clay. Use a tapered silicone tool to press the clay down and blend the joints together.

13 Mix some light pink buttercream with a little more liquid polymer clay to turn it into icing and use it to trace a few lines on the chocolate part of the strawberry.

14 To make the jam, mix red and translucent clay with a little liquid polymer clay and a little craft sand for texture. Then apply it directly into the hollow in a circular motion and quickly pull the tool away to create the overhanging peak. The jam needs to be quite firm for it to hold the shape while baking. Bake. Once cool, glaze the strawberry and jam with gloss varnish. Glaze the sponge too but apply a very small amount in a stippling motion to avoid getting a membrane-like finish.

15 Take a nail art drill and drill two holes, one on the bottom of the cupcake and one behind the strawberry. Add a couple of eye screw bails, strengthening the bond with cyanoacrylate glue.

Tip You could poke a headpin or wire into the cupcake and use an eyepin instead of eye screw bails, but you would need to rethink the position of the strawberry.

16 Using round- and flat-nose pliers, link a keyring to the top screw bail.

17 Using the same pliers, connect a spoon charm to the bottom screw bail using a jump ring.

10

13

16

Linzer Cookie Magnet

I LOVE IT WHEN MAKING THINGS OUT OF POLYMER CLAY FEELS JUST LIKE BAKING. SO, ROLL UP YOUR SLEEVES AND TIE ON YOUR APRON, BECAUSE IN THIS PROJECT WE'LL BE MAKING REPLICA LINZER COOKIES AND TURNING THEM INTO MAGNETS.

YOU WILL NEED

- Polymer clay in light brown (I used Premo in Raw Sienna), white, yellow, translucent, red and alizarin crimson (I used Premo)

- Soft pastels in beige

- Liquid polymer clay (I used FIMO Liquid)

- White or clear craft sand

- Acrylic paints in brown and white

- Craft magnet

- Cyanoacrylate glue

- Gloss and matte varnish

- Mini cheese grater

- Blade

- Pasta machine or rolling pin

- Cutter with scalloped edges

- Toothbrush

- Soft brush

- Dotting tool

- Round cutter

- Craft knife or small heart-shaped cutter

- Small paintbrush

- Sponge

1   Part-bake a piece of light brown polymer clay (see page 13). Once cool, grate it using the finest setting of a cheese grater. This is to create the effect from using ground almonds in real Linzer cookies. If the shavings are too big, chop them further with a blade.

Tip Remember to keep your polymer clay equipment separate from your kitchen utensils.

2   Take some white clay and mix it with a small amount of yellow and light brown to create a light beige colour to make the dough. Add some translucent clay to this mix. Mix in the shavings of light brown clay and put it through the thickest setting of your pasta machine. Use a round cookie cutter with scalloped edges to cut out the shape.

3   Texture the cookie with a toothbrush. If you find it tricky to get into the corners, cut some bristles off the toothbrush, secure the ends together with glue and use that to get into the small areas.

4   Cut a heart out of the centre of the cookie and texture the inside.

5   Take some beige soft pastel and dust it all around the edges of the cookie with a soft brush. Make another whole cookie and part-bake both.

6   Mix translucent polymer clay with some red and alizarin crimson. Roll out a sheet through the thickest setting of your pasta machine and cut out a circle that is smaller than the cookie.

7   Stick the circle to the baked and cooled cookie base using a little liquid polymer clay.

8   To make the jam, take the translucent red mix and mix it with liquid polymer clay. Add some white or clear craft sand to add some texture and make it look more like jam.

9 Use a dotting tool to spread the jam mix around the edge of the cookie, making sure that some of it goes on top of the red circle as well and that there are no gaps anywhere.

10 Add the top of the cookie, making sure the scalloped edges match. Part-bake.

11 Add some jam mix in the heart of the cookie; you can fill this up to the top or just add a bit. Bake.

12 Once your cookie is out of the oven and cool, take acrylic paint in warm brown and water it down a bit. Pick up a small amount of colour and apply it to the edges of the cookie, blending it towards the centre and/or blotting the excess with your fingers.

13 Apply the same wash on the sides of the cookie, then go back in with a small amount of pure paint, stippling it on the edges. This will create a beautiful contrast with the icing-sugar effect created in the next step.

14 Once all the brown paint is dry, take some white paint and a piece of sponge. Pick up some colour and blot away the excess so that only a residue is left on the sponge, then stipple it on the cookie to create the illusion of icing sugar.

Tip Test the amount of paint on a piece of paper before applying it to the cookie to make sure you don't have blobs of paint; it is easier to build up the colour than remove it.

15 When the paint is dry, stick a magnet to the back of the cookie with cyanoacrylate glue. Glaze the jam with gloss varnish and the cookie with matte varnish.

9

12

10

11

13

14

15

Neapolitan Cake Necklace

THIS IS THE PERFECT CAKE FOR THOSE WHO CAN'T DECIDE WHAT FLAVOUR THEY WANT MOST, AS IT COMBINES CHOCOLATE, STRAWBERRY AND VANILLA, WITH CREAM SANDWICHED IN BETWEEN. IT IS NOT ONLY FUN TO MAKE BUT THE RESULT IS SO PRETTY THAT IT MAKES AN ADORABLE NECKLACE.

YOU WILL NEED

- Polymer clay in dark brown (I used Premo in Burnt Umber), pink, translucent, Victoria sponge cake mix (see page 36), white, red and green

- Liquid polymer clay (I used FIMO Liquid)

- Miniature ceramic or polymer clay plate

- Miniature fork

- Acrylic paint in white

- Cyanoacrylate glue

- Screw eye bails

- Jump ring

- Necklace chain

- Gloss varnish

- Pasta machine or rolling pin

- Round cutter

- Craft knife/blade

- Toothbrush

- Needle tool

- Small paintbrush

- Nail art hand drill

- Round- and flat-nose pliers

1 Take polymer clay in dark brown, pink mixed with some translucent, and Victoria sponge cake mix and roll the sheets through the thickest setting of your pasta machine. Cut out a circle of each, browning the vanilla mix if desired (see page 18). Stack the colours in any order you want, sandwiching circles of white polymer clay in between them.

2 Cover the sides of the cake in a thin sheet of white polymer clay (setting #9 of your pasta machine) to create the illusion of a crumb coat.

3 Cut out a circle of white polymer clay to cover the top of the cake and blend it with your fingers.

4 Cut the cake into slices with a craft knife or blade.

5 Take a miniature plate and dab a little liquid polymer clay on it, then press a slice of cake on it.

6 Using a craft knife or a small cutter, remove chunks of cake to make it look part-eaten.

7 Texture the bottom of the cake with a toothbrush so that it looks spongy.

8 Use a needle tool to texture the sponge, also teasing the white clay a little. Part-bake.

9 Dab a little liquid polymer clay on a miniature fork and push it into the trimmings of cake. Then use a needle tool to texture it.

Tip If using a plastic fork, glue on a piece of textured cake after baking it.

10 To make the pineberry, take a little red clay and shape it into a teardrop. Flatten it slightly and use a needle to create the effect of the seeds. Add small pieces of green clay to make the leaves. Part-bake (see page 13).

1

4

8

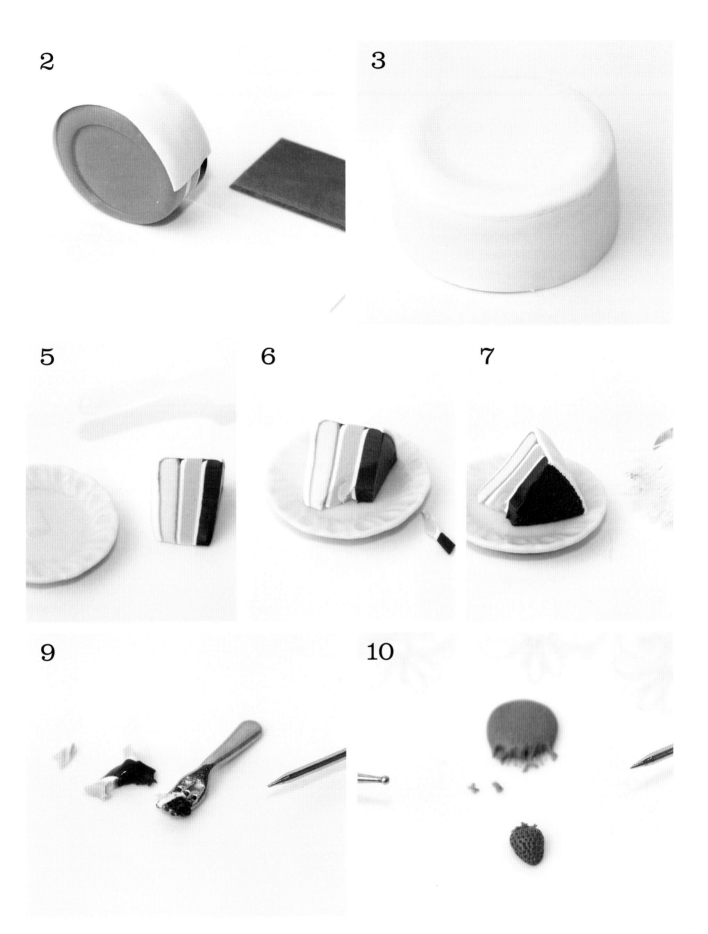

11 Once baked and cool, dry brush a little white acrylic paint on it. Let it dry.

12 Take the cake slice and remove it from the plate. Dab a little cyanoacrylate glue on the bottom and glue it back on. Polymer clay doesn't stick to ceramic or glass very well, so it needs to be glued in place if making jewellery and accessories.

13 Make some pink cream (see page 22), spread it on the cake and add the pineberry.

14 Make some white icing and add it to create the illusion that a fork has been dragged through it. Bake the cake and fork.

15 Once cool, use a small hand drill to make a hole in the back of the cake.

16 Brush a small amount of cyanoacrylate glue on a screw eye bail and screw it into the hole. Let dry.

17 Dab a little glue on the fork and bond it in place.

18 Using round- and flat-nose pliers, attach a jump ring to the screw eye bail.

19 Slide the necklace chain through the jump ring, and the necklace is complete.

11

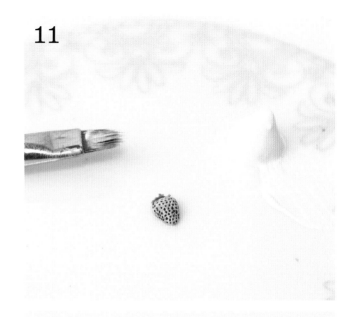

14

17

12

13

15

16

18

19

French Macaron Keyring

MAKING FRENCH MACARONS IS A FUN AND INTUITIVE WAY TO PLAY WITH COLOURS AND EFFECTS. IN THIS PROJECT I WILL SHOW YOU HOW TO MAKE A REPLICA MARBLED MACARON AND TURN IT INTO A KEYRING SO YOU CAN ALWAYS CARRY THIS CHIC PARISIAN TREAT WITH YOU.

YOU WILL NEED

- Polymer clay in light pink, fuchsia, yellow, mint, lavender and white (or any other colours you like)

- Decorations such as nail caviar

- Headpin or jewellery wire

- Liquid polymer clay (I used FIMO Liquid)

- Bead

- Keychain

- Gloss varnish

- Pasta machine or rolling pin

- Craft knife/blade

- Cling film

- 2½in (5cm) round cutter

- Needle tool

- Detail tool

- Toothpick

- Jewellery pliers: flat-nose, round-nose and side cutters

1. Roll out thin strands of polymer clay in light pink, fuchsia, yellow, mint and lavender, varying them in size depending on how much you want of each colour. Darker colours tend to overpower, so you might want to compensate by adding fewer of these or using more of the lighter colours.

2. Press all the strands together to secure them in place and turn them into a single cylinder.

3. Roll and stretch the cylinder, then fold it in half.

4. Twist the cylinder, securing the two pieces in place, and roll it again.

5. Repeat this two or three times; beyond this, the colours will start to blend together.

6. Scrunch up the cylinder.

7. Roll the clay into a ball until it is smooth.

8. Use your fingers to press out the clay into a pancake shape. This will make it easier to put through the pasta machine and avoid the clay tearing if it is too thick (or picking up loose bits of clay that may be lurking inside it).

9. Put the clay through your pasta machine, starting from the thickest setting and working your way to #3 or #4. Put the clay through without folding it, as you don't want to blend the colours further. The difference in temperature or consistency may result in some of the clay separating when put through the pasta machine, resulting in a gorgeous crackling effect.

10. Put some fuchsia polymer clay through the thickest setting of your pasta machine, cut out a piece for the base of the macaron shell and place it on an oven-safe dish. I like to slightly fold the piece in the middle when placing it on the dish, and then press the clay from the centre outwards to avoid trapping air.

1
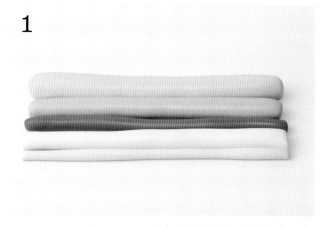

5

11. Place the marbled sheet on top of the fuchsia sheet and give it a little push to secure it and minimize the risk of getting air bubbles. You may want to cut the marbled sheet into sections to make this step easier.

12. Lay a piece of cling film on the clay, making sure it is tight so as not to get unwanted lines on the clay. Smooth the clay down and push it to avoid air bubbles. Then use a round cutter to cut out the shape.

13. Remove the cling film and excess clay and, using a needle tool, trace a line along the middle of the macaron shell.

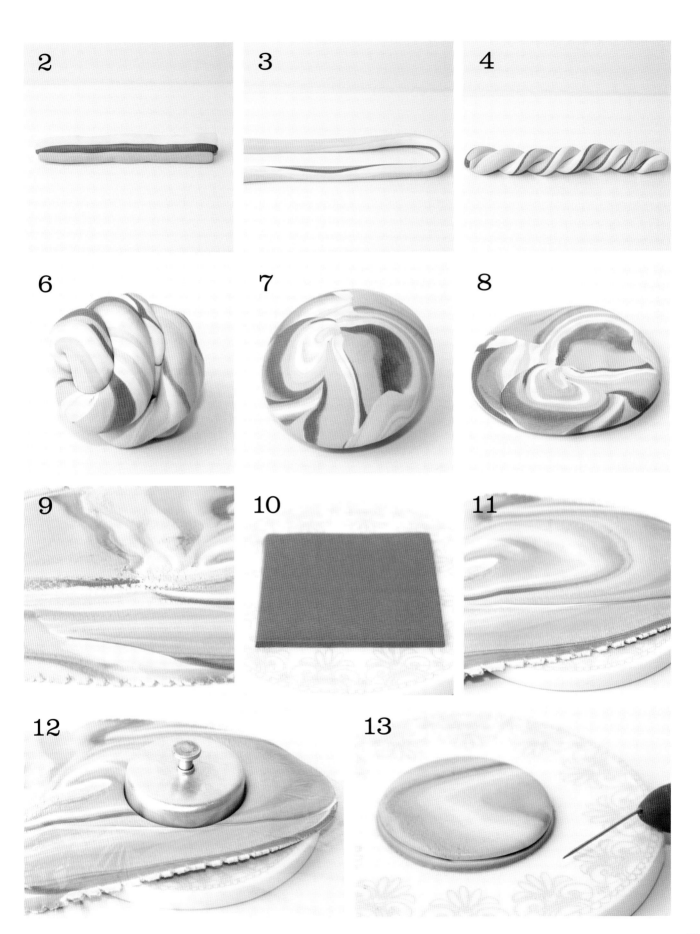

14 Use a toothpick in a stippling motion to texture the feet of the macaron shell. Make another macaron shell and part-bake for 10 minutes (see page 13).

Tip Varying the size of the holes will result in a more realistic look. I poke deeper holes here and there, especially underneath the line, as it gives the illusion of continuity that you can't achieve just with superficial holes.

15 Once cool, make some light vanilla icing mix (see page 22) from white and a little yellow polymer clay and drag it on one of the macaron shells (or both) in any pattern you like.

16 Add some decorations such as sprinkles using nail caviar or something of your choice. Part-bake for 15–20 minutes.

17 Roll some mint clay into a ball. Make a slit and push a headpin into the clay, closing the slit and blending the clay.

Tip Use a piece of wire if you don't have a headpin: bend it into an 'L' shape first, so it doesn't slide out of the clay.

18 Once the macaron shells are baked and cool, brush a little liquid polymer clay on the inside so that the uncured clay sticks.

19 Place the ball of mint clay with the headpin in the centre of a macaron shell and add the other one on top. Hold the macaron with both hands so that your thumbs are on the bottom and your other fingers on top, then gently apply even pressure throughout to result in an evenly spread filling.

20 Turn the macaron as you squeeze so you can keep an eye on the filling. Stop squeezing once the filling has reached the edges. Bake.

21 Slide a bead onto the wire and take the macaron by the base of the headpin with flat-nose pliers. Use your finger to push the wire over the pliers into a 90-degree angle.

22 Hold the wire with round-nose pliers in a vertical position so you can wrap it around the pliers.

23 Keep going past the macaron to complete the circle and create an eye.

24 Hold the eye with flat-nose pliers and wrap the rest of the wire around the neck two or three times.

25 Trim the excess wire with side cutters and close the loose end with flat-nose pliers.

26 Link the macaron to a keychain and glaze the macaron shells to give them a little sheen if desired. Let it dry completely.

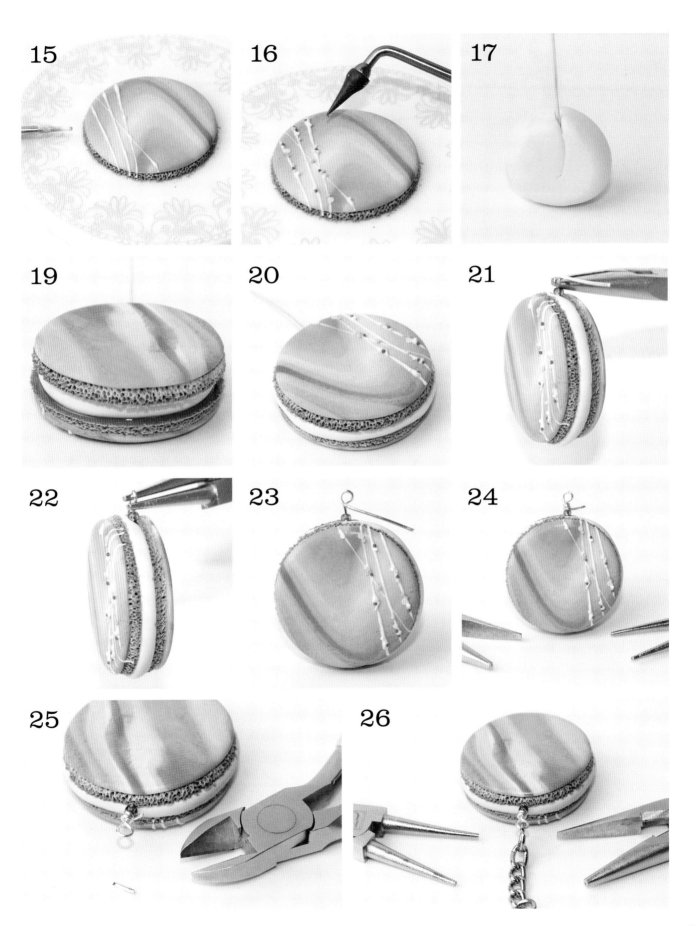

SUPPLIERS

Polymer Clay General Tools and Materials
www.amazon.co.uk
www.clayaround.com
www.cooksongold.com
www.craftmill.co.uk
www.ebay.co.uk
www.etsy.com
www.hobbycraft.co.uk
www.pencils4artists.co.uk

Miniature Crockery and Accessories
www.minimumworld.com
www.mytinyworld.co.uk

Fragrance Oils
http://www.craftastik.co.uk

Jewellery Findings
www.beadsdirect.co.uk
www.beadsunlimited.com
www.cooksongold.com
www.jewellerymaker.com
www.the-beadshop.co.uk

ACKNOWLEDGEMENTS

To my editor/Saint Sara, for being the most patient person on the planet, for your kindness and hard work. To my publishing team, for their amazing work and for making one of my dreams come true. To my dad, for believing in me, always. To my mother-in-law, for giving me my first blocks of polymer clay. To my fiancé Alex, for your love and for everything you've done for me. You are my rock. To my admirers all around the world, for their huge, huge hearts.

To Angie Scarr and Karen Pasieka, who introduced me to the art of making polymer clay canes and flowers respectively. To Patrizia Cozzo, Tanja Jensen and Stephanie Kilgast, to name but a few, whose passion, talent and uniqueness capture me. And to so many other artists outside the field of polymer clay, who inspire me through their work and humanity.

INDEX

First published 2019 by
Guild of Master Craftsman Publications Ltd
Castle Place, 166 High Street, Lewes, East Sussex, BN7 1XU, UK

ISBN 978 1 78494 537 4

Publisher Jonathan Bailey
Production Manager Jim Bulley
Senior Project Editor Sara Harper
Editor Nicola Hodson
Managing Art Editor Gilda Pacitti
Art Editor Cathy Challinor
Photographer Sara Morris
Step photography Maive Ferrando

Colour origination by GMC Reprographics
Printed and bound in China

To order a book, or to request a catalogue, contact:

GMC Publications Ltd, Castle Place, 166 High Street, Lewes,
East Sussex, BN7 1XU, UK
Tel : +44(0)1273 488005

www.gmcbooks.com